LIBERTY OR BONDAGE?

by Leona Hennessee

Foreword by Iverna Tompkins

Distributed by

Bridge Publishing, Inc.
South Plainfield, New Jersey 07080

LIBERTY OR BONDAGE?
Copyright © 1982 by Leona Hennessee
All Rights Reserved
Printed in the United States of America
Library of Congress Catalog Card Number: 82-72006
International Standard Book Number: 0-88270-531-8
Distributed by Bridge Publishing, Inc., South Plainfield, NJ 07080

Acknowledgments

I wish to thank all who had a hand in the preparation of this book. Especially to my husband, Dennis, for his long hours of help and encouragement.

To those who were gracious enough to give their time and constructive criticism in reading the manuscript: Dr. Ashcroft, Campbell McAlpine, Dr. Buddy Hicks, Don Phillips, and Iverna Tompkins.

A special thanks to the many involved in typing, correcting and copying. Last, but equal in importance, a special thanks to Dan and Pat O'Rear for their valuable help in editing and final typing.

Thank you, and God richly bless you all.

Contents

Preface

Our Heritage—Our Roots

For whatever was thus written in former days was written for our instruction. (Rom. 15:4 TAB)

I believe very much that the Old Testament covenant promises are the roots and heritage of all whose faith and trust are in Christ Jesus our Lord. Every believer becomes an inheritor of the covenant promises given to Abraham, Isaac, and Jacob.

God made a covenant thousands of years ago with Abraham. In this covenant—or agreement—Abraham promised to obey God and to follow Him wherever He led. God promised to lead and help and protect Abraham. He promised to be God, not only to Abraham but also to his descendants. He promised to provide him with a son to carry on the terms of the covenant, and He promised him an inheritance of land as an everlasting possession for him and his descendants.

God established Abraham's descendants as the Hebrew people, and through them He sent His Son Jesus, who not only reaffirmed the covenant promises but extended them to all the world. In essence, these promises are the expression of God's desire to have a relationship with people. He chose Abraham to begin that relationship. The relationship, the covenant, and the promises continued through Abraham's son, Isaac, and through Isaac's son, Jacob. The covenant was passed on through the generations to the cross of Calvary, where Jesus died for all of sinful mankind (Gal. 3:16, 22, 29).

Each of us who, by believing in Jesus Christ, has a relationship with God, is joined to God's covenant with Abraham and inherits the promises:

Consider Abraham: "He believed God, and it was credited to him as righteousness." Understand, then, that those who believe [us] are children of Abraham. The Scripture foresaw that God would justify the Gentiles [all those who are not Jews] by faith, and announced the gospel in advance to Abraham: "All nations will be blessed through you." So those who have faith [in Jesus as God's only Son] are blessed along with Abraham, the man of faith. (Gal. 3:6-8, NIV)

When God told Abraham he would be the father of "many nations," He included those of us who would believe and by faith receive the salvation of the Lord Jesus Christ.

Preface

In the books of Genesis and Exodus we see our beginnings and find our roots, the roots and beginnings of a spiritual journey to possess the land of our inheritance. For us, "possessing the land" is possessing our own lives for the Lord.

> Each one of you should know how to possess [control, manage] his own body [in purity, separated from things profane, and] in consecration and honor. (1 Thess. 4:4, TAB)

As I studied Genesis and Exodus, the Lord showed me how the struggles of the Hebrew nation to possess their inheritance parallels our battle to possess our lives for the Lord. The Hebrews had to possess their land over the opposition of the other peoples living there. As born-again believers we struggle against our own besetting attitudes and habits.

We have areas where our tempers are short. We run out of patience with those around us. We get irritated by the weaknesses we see in ourselves and others. We fall into attitudes of envy, malice, resentment and hatred. These attitudes are areas to possess, that is, to learn to control and manage—not only the wrong inner attitudes but also the unhealthy outward habits that we form because of them.

I'm sure we all can relate to some outward habit

that strokes our wrong inner attitudes. One is overeating. Does that jog your mind in the right direction?

As born-again believers, we struggle to come into the fullness of God's abundant, victorious life. My experience as a counselor and pastor has revealed that the majority of believers do not come into this possession. This inheritance (His victory in our lives over these attitudes and habits) is entirely our own; we need only reach out a hand and claim it.

One Scripture that really came alive to me was 1 Thess. 5:23. I believe it expresses the desire of the Father's heart for all who believe: that at the coming of the Lord we would be made blameless in spirit, soul and body. To me the possession of the land represents the possession of our souls and bodies in a spiritual walk with the Lord.

It is within my soul—that part of me in which my mind, my emotions, and my will reside—that constant battles rage. My mind produces runaway thoughts and imaginings. Imagination says my husband doesn't love or understand me (or that the man's wife doesn't understand him, or child and parent, or employee and boss, or vice versa). My thoughts and imaginings in turn affect my emotions. Then my will comes into focus and dictates certain orders to my body. That's where the stroking, or lack of it, comes in. On the one hand, we may say in effect, "If you do not love me or understand me, I'll get back at you," and form some habit, usually destructive, such as overeating, drugs or sexual vices. On the other hand, the same kinds of morally or physically destructive habits may speak with a voice that says to us, "That's all right; I love you, and you can do anything that makes you feel happy—feel good—feel fulfilled."

To possess the land is to control and manage the mind (by renewing it), the emotions (by forgiveness—letting go of resentment), and the free will. Those security habits are stopped, and the body is set free.

In this book we will take a close look at the mistakes of those who have walked the road before us. With God as our helper we need not repeat them. We see that on their journey out of Egypt (bondage) toward the promised land (their liberty) the Israelites, hard of hearing when God was speaking, continually looked back and desired again their bondage.

The Lord Jesus desires that each of us believers would come out of our sinful bondages (attitudes and habits) and into His glorious liberty. Soon we discover that we too are looking back, still desiring our bondages (that old way of life) instead of His liberty. Hence our subtitle, "You give *liberty*, Lord; why do I choose *bondage?*" Why do we choose to keep our souls in bondage to a short temper, a raunchy disposition, fears, worry, and tormented thoughts? We can be liberated. We can be free.

About the Author

I remember the first time I met Leona Hennessee; I was at the end of my rope. She greeted me with an outstretched hand, and I saw that "I understand" look in her eye when she said, "I'm praying for you." I didn't even know she knew I had a problem. That's the way it has been for the past seventeen years in my acquaintance with Leona. She has been able to minister healing to me when I didn't even know I was sick (not always in the most pleasant way, however). She is the most straightforward, direct friend a person could have, holding no punches but displaying the most established, persistent love that only a life deeply embedded in Christ Jesus could share.

Through the many trials (blessings) of learning to walk with the Lord into a God-called teacher/prophet ministry coupled with being a wife for thirty years, mother of three and grandmother, Leona has received much instruction and comfort from the Lord. Her mission now is to teach and comfort others that they might come to know the heavenly Father in an intimate, personal relationship and be presented a bride fit for King Jesus.

Pat Severson
Director of Mobile Ministries

Foreword

This is a book which will benefit believers of all maturity levels. Even the difficult-to-accept parts (i.e. "wives, submit") are tempered with the balance of promise. I recommend it to pastors and counselors for a practical approach to counseling and to both men and women as an aid to freedom.

Iverna M. Tompkins

Introduction

After a day of counseling, dinner out with my husband, Dennis, is a treat I look forward to. His first words when he comes home at night often are: "What's going on around here?" This question lets me know he loves me and is interested in my day. Dennis is an electrical engineer; he tracks satellites. He has also been "engineering" my life for thirty years, helping me to become a very disciplined person. By teaching me discipline, he has released me to a God-called ministry, a ministry which demands time for writing, for teaching, and for studying. Dennis' profession also demands time, often overtime, and time on the night shift. Sometimes we greet each other with a quick "Hi" and an immediate "Goodbye," so when we go out to dinner together, it is a time we can catch up on "what's going on." These are really special times.

This book began to emerge one evening as we were having dinner together. As we waited for a table, one thought kept popping into my mind—you know, one of those thoughts we can't push out of our minds after a day at work. My last counselee's heavy burden made me keep thinking, "Why do we chose our bondages—those attitudes, habits and dispositions—rather than the liberty Jesus provided?" Dennis and I talked awhile about us as human beings and about how difficult it is for some to choose freedom from old life patterns and habits.

As we were seated, my mind drifted back to my last counseling session. There a young woman had sat across from me and expressed how she felt about the myriad troubles confronting her. Mary (not her real name) is the mother of three children and the wife of an unbelieving husband. She feels she married the wrong man, and she has an imagined relationship with the man she thinks she should have married. She says her husband loves her, but he is distant. He has no desire to discipline the children or to assume leadership in the household. As a result, Mary thinks negative thoughts toward her husband continually.

She needed to see that her thoughts and inner attitudes can cause a partner to react by being distant. She needed to change her attitude—to control and manage it. She let me know right away that Christ Jesus was very much a part of her life, as was the reading of her Bible. Then came that big word "but" we find being expressed by so many people. This young lady declared herself a born-again believer whose only hope was in Jesus, but she lived a defeated, passive life, a roller-coaster existence. Why?

Just then the "Tostado Especial" arrived. So did the title of the book. I asked Dennis what he thought of the title, *Liberty or Bondage?* He didn't think the title would give him an overwhelming desire to dive right in and start reading. So, to elaborate, I added the subtitle: "You Give Me Liberty, Lord—Why Do I Choose Bondage?" Dennis became a little more responsive and began to have ideas of his own (he has since become my rewrite man and greatest encourager). At least he didn't just say, "Pass the taco sauce" to change the subject.

That young woman's burden helped motivate me to write. The substance of this book is what I have learned from God's Word. Recently I finished an extensive study in the book of Exodus. I found a real similarity between the Israelites and so many in the body of believers today. The Israelites had family and social problems too. God was leading them, His chosen people, on a journey to a promised land. We, as believers in Christ as our Savior and Lord, became part of a large family, the body of believers. We have our family and social problems, but we too are a chosen people unto God. God, through the Holy Spirit, is leading us to a promised land—our spiritual inheritance (Col. 1:12).

In Exodus we find the Hebrews living in Egypt. God has chosen them to become a great nation, and He had promised to be their God. The Hebrews (or Israelities, as they were now called), had become a great nation. In spite of severe servitude, hardships and trials, they had multiplied, from the seventy descendants of Abraham, Isaac and Jacob, to a family of three million. Suffering under very cruel and hard taskmasters, they cried out to God to deliver them from their bondage. God heard, and He sent them a deliverer—Moses.

Any difference for us as fallen mankind? As unbelievers we were in bondage to sin and self, and God sent us a deliverer—Jesus.

Well, Moses came along and said, "Hey gang, we're getting out of here and going to a land flowing with milk and honey, big enough to hold us all. No taskmasters to rule you and make you slaves, only a loving God to lead the way!"

You know the story. The Lord, through Moses, inflicted several plagues on the Egyptians, forcing them to set His people free. "Hurray!!! We're on our way to freedom and liberty!!"

They didn't get very far before they discovered that liberty and freedom had some drawbacks. When they came up against a big sea in front of them with the enemy hot on their trail, their minds suddenly and unanimously drew a blank. They forgot all God had done to get them out of their slavery. They forgot that the powerful hand of God had caused things to happen in Egypt— water turning to blood, frogs everywhere, gnats, flies, livestock sick to death, boils, hail, locusts, darkness in the daytime for three days, and finally the death of all firstborn sons.

The people knew it was God who had done all these wonders, signs, and miracles to the Egyptians. In Egypt, God made a separation between the Israelites and the Egyptians. The Israelites suffered only the first three plagues. After that they did not go through the experiences the Egyptians did. Now, at the Red Sea, they were being totally and personally affected. They were afraid.

Where was God? As they stood in front of that body of water with the enemy bearing down on them, they cried out, "Was it because there were no graves in Egypt that you brought us to this desert to die?" (Hadn't they lived through all the plagues without death touching one of them?) "What have you done to us by bringing us out of Egypt? Didn't we say to you in Egypt, 'Leave us alone; let us serve the Egyptians'? It would have been better for us to serve the Egyptians than to die in the desert!" (Exod. 14:10-12 NIV).

Well, Moses had to convince all the people, "Hey, really now, it might not look like it at this moment, but God does love you, and He has a perfect plan for your life." God brought them through the Red (or Reed) Sea on dry land, eliminated the enemy, and began to lead them through the desert. How their hearts rejoiced in God their Savior! They sang:

> Your right hand, O Lord, was majestic in power. Your right hand, O Lord, shattered the enemy. . . . Who among the gods is like you, O Lord? Who is like you—majestic in holiness, awesome in glory, working wonders?
>
> In your unfailing love you still lead the people you have redeemed. In your strength you will guide them to your holy dwelling. (Exod. 15:6, 11, 13)

That was yesterday, Lord, and that was all fine, *but* today is a different story. What about my stomach? After all Lord, in Egypt we might have been slaves but at least we have our flesh pots (Exod. 16:2, 4). Did you bring us out here only to starve us?

Again the Lord shows His mercy and love, but He tests the Israelites to see if they can learn to *listen* and *obey*. That seems to be the problem. Can't we, each of us who are believers, have *liberty* without having to listen and obey?

Introduction

As Dennis and I finished our dinner, the ideas were taking shape. We are like the children of Israel. Sometimes we find it very hard to listen and obey. The Lord Jesus Christ has redeemed us by the shedding of His blood to free us from our bondages of sin and self. Why, like our predecessors the Israelites, do we constantly feel that God has brought us this far just to kill us, afflict us, try us and fry us? If that's love, surely bondage was better!

In the following pages we hope to better understand the liberty we believers have in Jesus—the benefits as well as the responsibilities to listen and obey. In this book we will take a look at the Israelites; we hope we will learn from their mistakes. We see that on their journey out of Egypt (bondage) to the promised land (their liberty) the hard-headed Israelites continually looked back and desired again their bondage (their old way of life).

The Lord Jesus desires that each of us believers would come out of our sinful bondages (attitudes, dispositions and habits) and into His glorious liberty. Soon we discover that we too are looking back, still desiring our bondages (old life styles) instead of His liberty. Hence, our subtitle, "You give *liberty*, Lord, why do I choose *bondage?*" Why do we choose these soulish (mental, emotional and willful) bondages over spiritual liberty?

1

What Is Our Liberty?

Liberty is defined as "freedom from oppression, tyranny, or domination. The state or condition of being free, as from confinement; release from bondage or slavery."

In your life have you become aware of more bondage to than freedom from oppression, anxiety, fears, runaway thoughts, attitudes that build up inside, causing resentment, anger, hostility, hate, etc.?

I do believe our first requisite for liberty is a personal relationship with our Lord Jesus Christ. He is our only source of hope and help. By a personal relationship with Jesus I mean our faith in His death for our sins, His resurrection from the dead for our victorious life, and His being seated in the heavenlies, ever interceding before the Father in our behalf. To me, our peace that passes all understanding is embodied in this one fact: that Jesus is ever before the Father reminding Him, "Father, she might have blown it today, but

1

look—she's penitent, and remember—it was for *her* sins that I died."

Why do we so easily become prey to defeat, unbelief, murmuring and complaining, living like we are on one big roller coaster ride? Do we have a misconception of Christianity that makes us slaves to an up-and-down existence? The children of Israel, when they left Egypt, had a picture in mind of what they thought liberty was for them. Can you picture it? A rose-covered path (without thorns), with sweet fragrances, little girls running to and fro with flower baskets, dropping rose petals along the way. Glimmering streams of water, tall pines, green meadows. Banqueting tables set before them interspersed along the way. And then this kindly grandfather figure meeting them from Mount Sinai giving all kinds of love and warm embraces.

What shook them up were the barren desert, no food (except that awful manna), sometimes no water, and that constant walking. God even had the nerve to make a decree regarding the manna, to test them. He said, *"If you will diligently hearken to the voice of the Lord your God, and will do what is right* in His sight and will listen to and obey His commandments and keep all His statutes, I will put none of the diseases upon you which I brought upon the Egyptians"* (Exod. 15:26, TAB, italics mine).

That was the crux of the matter, the monkey

wrench in the works. They did not want the testing. They did not want to have to listen carefully and to obey. They wanted no decrees to follow. They just wanted the rose-covered path straight to the Promised Land.

As a counselor, I meet many in my office who have that same problem. Somehow they received the idea that becoming a Christian was a rose-covered path to heaven, hassle-free, without any listening or obeying required. After all, Jesus paid the debt that made me free, and now I'm covered by His grace. The Father doesn't see me; He sees Jesus, and I'm clothed in His righteousness.

Now there is a truth here that cannot be denied: Jesus *did* pay the debt, and salvation is "not of works lest any man should boast" (Eph. 2:9). I am clothed in His righteousness. But He still requires me to listen carefully to His Word and to become a doer and not just a hearer. I am required to come into *obedience*. Even Jesus was required to obey the Father (Heb. 5:8).

Obedience is still the bugaboo, the culprit. "Oh Lord, not me, you mean the preachers, the teachers, the elders and deacons, but not me, Lord." The children of Israel were told that if you "will *listen* to and obey His commandments and keep all His statutes, I will put none of the diseases upon you" (Exod. 15:26, TAB).

Those who come to our office suffering

3

emotionally, mentally and sometimes physically from numerous difficulties—fears, anxiety attacks, mental depression, sleeplessness, etc.—are looking for a way out. Yet they resist having the *listening* ear and an *obedient* heart attitude. God requires a change in our behavior. He does give us commandments.

We have a commandment to love others as Jesus loved us. That's not always so easy. One wife and mother seemed to think this was required only when love was coming her way. She had a husband who did not know how to express his love. He seemed hostile and unappreciative, even distant, so much of the time. This wife developed an attitude of resentment toward his many demands. She expressed it this way: "These demands are always top riority, and if one slip occurs I face his wrath." Usually an onslaught of verbal abuse was included. He would say she was stupid, that she had no common sense, that she was incapable of doing anything right or of ever pleasing him. She became very depressed and cried most of the time. She developed an ulcer and could not sleep at night. She finally came for counseling in order to relieve these symptoms. She wanted a way out of sleeplessness, depression, ulcers and anxiety attacks.

After some time of questioning her relationships with the Lord Jesus, her husband, her children and her family, she came to a place of realizing that she had to listen to God's Word and obey. She must forgive her husband's inadequacy. After receiving God's forgiveness, she reached out to her husband. She stopped feeling sorry for herself that her need for love was not being fulfilled. She began to see *his* need for love also. The hostility did not immediately disappear in her husband, and there were still times of tears. After releasing herself to the Lord and allowing the Lord to love her husband through her, she began to sleep peacefully at night. Her ulcer disappeared, along with the anxiety attacks and depression. Her focus had changed. She no longer just wanted love constantly coming her way. She became a giver, pressed down and running over; she gave love away. She then reaped the consequences; her husband was soon set free to love.

By the time a counselee and I get to the root or core of a problem, the situation is the same. The person has regarded the bondage—resentment, rage, hurt feelings, self-pity, ulcers, hives, sleepless nights—as better than having to pay the price of obedience—the way that leads to liberty.

Does Liberty Cost Me Something?

Liberty was expressed as freedom from bondage and slavery to attitudes which cause physical and mental damage. Maybe you ask, "If Jesus paid the price for my freedom, what then is it going to cost me? What is the price?" The Lord expressed the price as the death of self and self-centeredness.

We are born self-centered. As we become adults, some of us do not shed that self-centered shell, which hardens with age. It develops even deeper into self-love, self-righteousness, self-gratification, etc., until we are locked in.

In our society, modern psychology teaches us the humanistic point of view that man is not responsible for his own behavior. We are taught that our behavior was fashioned by faulty parents with wrong ideas, by peer pressure, by cultural influences, and so forth. Supposedly, because of all this outside influence, it's all right to blame others for our apparent weaknesses.[1] This so-called modern idea is not so modern, however. In the book of Genesis we see Adam saddled with the same problem. Our first parents fell short when they sinned through disobedience (there's that word again). God said,

Adam, I want you to pay close attention now, because I'm going to tell you something. I've made you a beautiful world to live in, with a garden that has everything you need. I gave you authority and dominion over every-

---

[1] Jay Adams, *Competent to Counsel.*

thing and even let you name all the animals. I saw you were lonely and even made from your rib a companion. But one thing I ask. Don't eat of the tree of the knowledge of good and evil, for the day you do you will surely die. (Gen. 2:7-17, Leona's paraphrased version).

That was no small command; death is a big thing to face. Well, Eve got curious and ate; Adam followed suit. When the Lord came to talk with them that night in the cool of the evening, He found them hiding. To His question, "why are you hiding?" Adam answered, "Why am I hiding! That woman you gave me caused me to sin." He blamed Eve. Eve blamed the serpent, and we've been blaming others ever since.

Now, part of the price for liberty is honesty and truthfulness, and it must be paid before anything can be accomplished in my life, personally, or in yours.

David states:

For I am conscious of [acknowledge] my transgressions; [He admits his own responsibility for his sin. As king, he didn't blame his mother, political pressures, his wife, or the devil.] my sin is ever before me. . . . Behold, You [Lord] desire truth in the inner being; make me therefore to know wisdom in my inmost heart. (Ps. 51:3, 6 TAB)

The young lady I mentioned at the beginning of this chapter was just one of many who expressed the same problem: "I know the Lord died for me, and He loves me, but He seems so distant. Sometimes I feel like He doesn't even exist, or care, or hear my prayers. I'm always blowing it!"

The greatest temptation we believers have is to become discouraged. We come into our relationship with the Lord happy, with childlike faith and new-found zeal. We start praying for our loved ones (husbands, wives, children, etc.). Trials come, and things seem to go from bad to worse. "God, why aren't you answering my prayers?" This question plagues us and doubts set in. Discouragement overwhelms us. We seem less eager to read God's Word and to seek Him in prayer. Old habits loom up before us, and it seems we turn to food, liquor, drugs, sweets, etc., again for comfort and solace. Our mind tells us we are not getting solace from the Lord. The old nature pulls us because we feel God must have let us down.

We need to realize that our Father does hear our prayers for those loved ones. When tests come, it isn't because He does not love us or hear us. He knows our heart and desires; the desire of the Father is also for their salvation. Even our desires and prayers need the fiery test. We need to realize, as the Father does, that even our desires and prayers sometimes start from selfish, impure motives. Does an unsaved husband make life difficult? Do I want salvation for him so that my life will be better and more hassle-free, or so that he will have a personal relationship with the Lord? The Lord tests us because of His great love for all concerned. Do I want my child saved and off drugs just so peace will return? Do I pray for my boss just so he can change his raunchy disposition? Where do my motives lie? The answer to this question determines the extent of discouragement and turning to self. When I am assured that it is true that God is "not willing that any should perish, but that all should come to repentance" (2 Pet. 3:9). I then come to peace with the testings and learn from them. I rest in the fact that His mighty power is at work within us to accomplish His desires, plans and purposes for each of us. Then discouragement will not lead me away from total trust in my Father, God. Old ways and habits will not have such a great pull.

These self-made bondages are very real to the ones oppressed and enslaved by them. I'm discovering more and more that the bondages are a form of security that we choose. If we continue to have an ulcer or some other physical or mental problem, attention does come our way. Not so much is required of us. We have an excuse to be pitied.

In his honest confession to the Lord, David

asked the Lord to teach him wisdom in his inmost being. That is, as we said earlier, a great part of the price of liberty. The question still remains: why do we resist?

In our counseling sessions—in so many cases—the root or core of the problem of constantly failing and never quite being victorious, is an unwillingness to: (a) come to forgiveness, (b) let go of resentment, or (c) give up a bad attitude, whether it be jealousy, envy, criticism, etc. We seem to resist letting go of our roots and causes. (O Lord, please teach us your wisdom!)

So, another part of the price we pay is the giving up of the luxury of self-pity, thinking we are the only ones with this particular problem. "No one could understand because my problem is so unique." Does that sound familiar to you?

We really have to die to self in order to forgive others the wrongs they've done to us. This seems to be like pulling teeth without anesthetics. Since we are descendants of Adam, we all come under the curse of the disobedience in eating the fruit of the tree of the knowledge of good and evil, or rights and wrongs. It seems that since that day people have declared by their actions, "I am right to feel and act the way I do because of the wrong things you say and do to me. You have to change, and beg forgiveness, and then maybe my attitude toward you and my actions against you might change."

The hard part for us is the Lord's requirement. He said, "Forgive us our debts [sins], as we also have forgiven (left, remitted and let go the debts, and given up resentment against) our debtors. . . . For if you forgive people their trespasses—that is, their reckless and willful sins, leaving them, letting them go and giving up resentment—your heavenly Father will also forgive you. But if you do not forgive others their trespasses . . . neither will your Father forgive you your trespasses" (Matt. 6:12-15, TAB).

What is the hard part? Forgiving others when they do the wrong things to us and then don't even seem to care, notice, or be punished. That's the price none of us wants to pay. We want them to be caught and punished and to beg our forgiveness. We do not want to be the ones to have to forgive and forget. As an illustration:

A young woman constantly felt she could not love her husband as she desired to, and at times certain things he did and said caused her great depression (to the point of attempting suicide and possessing an almost loathsome hatred for him. She was a born-again believer, and she wanted the Lord to uncover the very root cause. After much prayer the Lord revealed to her a situation that was, to her, a terrifying experience. At age six, when she was at the movies, a trusted neighbor had been sent to pick her up. Instead of taking her right home, he took her down a dark alley to a dark garage and forced her into oral copulation. This experience had caused her problems as an adult with her husband. The Lord revealed other things hidden in her subconscious. Her brother would do such things as shooting her with a BB gun and catching snakes and spiders in a jar and throwing them on her as she walked by unaware. One day, on the way home from school, he threw a gunny sack over her head and rolled her down a hill.

All these things had been suppressed in her subconscious mind, but they affected her adult life in her relationship with her husband. As the Lord did the revealing, He also did some requiring. (You guessed it—forgiveness.)

She said, "The Lord seemed to reveal to me the time He hung on the cross. He was being unjustly put to death. He had done no wrong. In front of Him were taunting, angry, hateful people He had been only kind to. He had healed the sick, fed the multitudes, and gone about the land doing good. As He hung on the cross in agony, He spoke to the Father from His heart as He said, 'Father, forgive them; they don't know what they are doing to me. They don't realize the grief they've caused or the pain they personally are inflicting!' On my knees before the Lord I could understand how He felt. At that moment I prayed and said, 'Father, forgive that man for what he did to me; he did not know all the years of torturous nightmares he caused me to have. I forgive him too.' "

What reason did she have to forgive? The sin was done to her; what sin of hers would need forgiveness? The Lord said to forgive others, and He would forgive us our sins.

As a child, this young woman developed an attitude toward men, toward herself, and toward God. This attitude became a suppressed resentment of having been made female in the first place. Her thought was, "If God had not made me a woman, none of this would have happened." Actually, she had to come to the place of forgiving God for having created her. Her sins of resentment toward God, herself, and men were forgiven as she forgave those who had sinned against her. She paid the price for her liberty when she chose to take responsibility for her own adult behavior and actions. The price was dying to her own rights, to the self-pity that allowed what was done years ago to affect her adult actions and to keep her in captivity to hatred and resentment toward her husband and her own self.

She was able to reap the consequences of her new-found liberty and freedom from her own self-made prison. It was through honesty in the inner person that her price was paid. The resentment was gone, and a new love took its place. A love for God the Father became a deep reality for the first time because now there was no need to resent god.

When I first bring this concept of resenting God to the attention of many counselees, the thought sets them back on their heels. Not many of us trust our relationship with the Father enough to be honest and to admit that there is a possibility of resenting, blaming, or actually hating God. Those of us who have not come to claim and remain in a state of liberty may have as the root cause a resentment toward God that needs to be honestly faced, confessed, and dealt with, so that we can come into a new-found sense of liberty.

2

Understanding Self Leads Away From Bondage

Understanding ourselves is of major importance if we are to come out of our bondages—those attitudes, dispositions and habits unbecoming to us as Christians.

I remember the roller coaster days of my earlier Christian experience. One thing especially caused my ups and downs. My temper (along with my lack of patience and my irritability) was my bugaboo. In our church our pastor taught Galatians 5:22 and 23 with a fervor. He had us memorize these fruits of the Spirit:

> But the fruit of the Spirit is love, joy, peace, patience, kindness, goodness, faithfulness, gentleness and self-control. . . . (Gal. 5:22, 23 NIV)

I would recite these at Wednesday night Bible class and vow to let these fruits be in evidence in my life. Thursday morning would soon enough reveal that the fruits weren't being produced. Getting the husband off to work on time and the kids to school on time had a way of producing the opposite. Someone would complain about the breakfast (too cold), then the lunches (not another dry sandwich!); usually buttons came up missing so early in the morning. Holes crept into pockets or socks. The alarm didn't ring at the right time. Books were lost, reports not finished. I could never figure out why I was always the one to be blamed for these little calamities. Why was I the one who had instantly to make all wrongs right? Irritation came first. Hurt (crushed pride) usually brought tears, and temper followed. Why wasn't I loving, full of bubbly joy, conveying peace, patient and understanding, kind and gentle? Those were my downs. All day I would pray and work at these fruits—oh, would I climb to great spiritual heights! Then everyone came home, and I found myself slipping into "the downs" again.

My life has changed now, after years of trials applied by a loving Father so that the Holy Spirit could take control of my life and produce His fruit in me. I could not produce the fruit; He did.

At that time Paul and I were both in agreement with his expressions in Romans 7:

> I do not understand what I do. For what I want to do I do not do, but what I hate I do. . . .

16

I know that nothing good lives in me, that is, in my sinful nature. For I have the desire to do what is good, but I cannot carry it out. For what I do is not the good I want to do; no, the evil I do not want to do—this I keep on doing. Now if I do what I do not want to do, it is no longer I who do it, but it is sin living in me that does it. So I find this law at work: When I want to do good, evil is right there with me. For in my inner being [spirit] I delight in God's law; but I see another law at work in the members of my body, waging war against the law of my mind [soul] and making me a prisoner of the law of sin at work within my members. What a wretched man I am! Who will rescue me from this body of death? Thanks be to God—through Jesus Christ our Lord! (Rom. 7:15-25, NIV)

Paul just expressed our "roller coaster" ride for us, didn't he? Did that fit any of you where you are right now? What helped me was seeing that struggle of the new man vs. the old man, or the new nature vs. the old nature.

I believe we were created in the likeness and image of God our Father (Gen. 1:26). That likeness and image are tripartite. That likeness is not a physical one, for we know that God is spirit. He is not a material being. The image consists in righteousness, knowledge and holiness of truth; in intellectual and moral likeness rather than in a physical resemblance.[1] We are triune, because He is triune. He is God the Father (Spirit), God the Spirit (Soul), and God the Son (Body). Yet He is one God; we experience Him in three expressions.

There are some who do not agree with the concept of the Trinity. They do not believe that man is anything more than a dualistic or dichotomous being. According to Scripture, however, we are tripartite like our Father.

We read,

> May God himself, the God of peace, sanctify you through and through. May your whole *spirit, soul,* and *body* be kept blameless at the coming of our Lord Jesus Christ. (1 Thess. 5:23, NIV, italics mine)

I believe very much that we are triune persons, because God created us spirit, soul and body. With others there is no problem believing that we are spirit, soul and body; their problem comes in defining spirit and soul because they are so interconnected and interwoven. One explanation best fits us. It helped me to see that this endless problem has a solution. I quote Watchman Nee:

---

[1] William Evans, *The Great Doctrines of the Bible,* p. 20

Is it a matter of consequence to divide spirit and soul? It is an issue of supreme importance for it affects tremendously the spiritual life of the believer. How can a believer understand spiritual life if he does not know what is the extent of the realm of the spirit? Without such understanding how can he grow spiritually? To fail to distinguish between spirit and soul is fatal to spiritual maturity.[2]

As an illustration to picture ourselves as persons, let's use this simple circle diagram.

According to Watchman Nee, my spirit (inner man, new man) is comprised of:

God-Conscience—consciousness; God-Communion—fellowship; Intuition—knowing.

In my spirit, my inner man, I have that intimate relationship with my Savior and Lord through the Holy Spirit, now joined to mine.

---

[2]Watchman Nee, *Spiritual Man,* Vol. 1, p. 22.

My <u>soul</u> is that part of me that is my

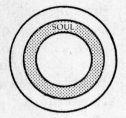

Intellect—mind, reasoning;
Emotions—feelings—love,
    hate, rage, etc.;
Will—volition—my free
    choices.

According to God's Word, man was formed from the dust of the earth. God breathed into his nostrils the breath of life, and he became a living soul. When the "breath of life" entered man it became man's spirit. In turn, the spirit in contact with man's body produced his soul.

Nee explains the relationship between spirit, soul and body:

The spirit cannot act directly upon the body. It needs a medium, and that medium is the soul produced by the touching of the spirit and the body, binding these two together. The spirit can subdue the body through the medium of the soul, so that it will obey God; likewise the body through the soul can draw the spirit into loving the world. . . .

The spirit transmits its thought to the soul and the soul exercises the body to obey the spirit's order. Before the fall of man the spirit controlled the whole being through the soul. Before man committed sin the power of the soul was completely under the dominion of the spirit. Its strength was therefore the spirit's strength.[3]

My body carries out the orders of my soul and consists of the senses of taste, touch, sight, smell and hearing, all influenced very much by the world around me.

When man was first created, he (Adam) was blessed with an intimate relationship with his heavenly Father. The Father would come into the garden in the cool of the evening and walk and talk with Adam.

In the cool of the evening God cummuned with man (Gen. 3:8). Adam was Spirit-led and Spirit-guided. The spirit of man was led by the Spirit of God. Adam received from God intuitive wisdom, knowledge and understanding, with which he could rule and have dominion over all the world and the animals. He could name all those animals and be right, because he had an inner ear that listened to all the wisdom of God. He could discern intuitively and know. He did not have to rely totally on his own limited reasoning ability.

---

[3]Watchman Nee, *Spiritual Man*, Vol. 1, pp. 26-27.

Intuitively, he had no limitations. As God's creation, he had no bounds.

Only when Adam fell did he become bound and limited. The only command Adam was given in his new world was not to eat of the tree of the "knowledge of good and evil" (Gen. 2:17). God told him that on the day he ate of that tree he would surely die. When Eve gave way to independence, curiosity and temptation, she and Adam both gave way to willful disobedience and ate of the fruit.

In Genesis 3, when God came to the garden and found them hiding, they were both still physically alive and well. But there had been a death; things were not the same. The light had gone out.

The Spirit of God was no longer leading and guiding Adam. He had lost his inner ear for that intuitive knowledge. That was the death and separation. God's Spirit could not be joined with man's fallen and sinful spirit. The sin of disobedience had caused a great gulf of separation, and the effects ran deep and became quite costly.

Man now had to turn to his own resources.

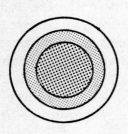 His soul would now have to lead and guide. He would have to rely on his own limited reasoning (intellect), which depended upon his own experiences. He was now bound to his emotions, which determined his choices, right or wrong.

In Genesis we see again how emotions helped govern choices. Adam had two sons born to him (also many other sons and daughters. These two are mentioned specifically because of the situation caused by their birth). Cain became jealous and envious of Abel because Abel obeyed god and was accepted by God. Abel, acknowledging man's fallen state, brought an animal sacrifice. He agreed with God that blood had to be shed to atone for man's sins. Cain brought his own produce, works of his own labors. He was coming to God on his own merits, admitting neither sin nor a need for a Savior.

Cain brought forth his own achievements and wanted acceptance without obedience. His emotions affected his attitude. He felt envy, anger, and then hatred. His emotions affected his thinking, so he chose to kill his obedient brother. He chose to kill because of how he felt. He did not make a right choice, and when confronted with what he had done he did not repent or feel sorry. He only became angry because he was banished and driven away from his surroundings. He did not repent of the sin of murder; he only became angry when he had to reap the consequences of that sin. (So many of us don't mind the sin; it's the consequences we dislike reaping.)

This is the state that man is still in today. It is for this reason that our Lord Jesus Christ said in John 3:3, 5, NIV:

Unless a man is born again. . . . Unless a man is born of water.

(This involves repentance, agreeing that we are fallen and sinful and that we need a Savior.)

and the Spirit,

(God's Spirit again joined with our spirit, making us alive again in our inner man, or reborn.)

he cannot enter the kingdom of God. Flesh gives birth to flesh,

(That stuck-in-the-soul, fallen state of mankind.)

but the Spirit gives birth to the spirit.

(That spirit that died at Adam's fall, that lies dormant until impregnated by God, the Holy Spirit, at our spiritual rebirth.)

While in this fallen state, as we noted earlier, we are controlled by our mind, our way of thinking affected by experiences and reasoning abilities gleaned over our years of learning and growing. Our mind, together with our emotions, determines our choices.

When we accept Jesus as our Lord and Savior, agreeing with Him that "all have sinned, and come short of the glory of God" (Rom. 3:23), when we realize that we have no merit of our own to claim, we are born again. At that moment, when we are born again, our spirit is made new, reborn. Now God's Holy Spirit lives in us.

> And you also were included in Christ when you heard the word of truth, the gospel of your salvation. Having believed, you were marked in him with a seal, the promised Holy Spirit, who is a deposit guaranteeing our inheritance until the redemption of those who are God's possession—to the praise of His glory. (Eph. 1:13-14)

Now when the spirit is alive we have access again intuitively to all the knowledge of God our Father. Hallelujah! Now we should be "sailing into Port Liberty." O, wretched man, where still lies my problem?

After all my years of control through my mind, will and emotion, I don't want to lose control. Who would I be? What would happen to me? The spirit of a newborn Christian is a baby, and who wants to turn over the control to a baby?

3

Problem Defined— Where to From Here?

In chapter one we saw that the price for our own liberty was paid through the shed blood of Jesus Christ who continually intercedes on our behalf. Yet the appropriation of this glorious liberty is realized only as we listen to the still, small voice of God's Holy Spirit and respond in obedience to His every command. We further learned that we must take responsibility for our own behavior and face the truth concerning our own inner feelings and attitudes. Giving up the luxury of self-pity and resentment, we must repent, die to self, and allow God's forgiveness and healing to release us into the liberty already secured for us by His Son.

Yet all of this is just an ideal unless we understand ourselves as God created us. In chapter two we looked at the relationship between spirit, soul and body and learned that in the process of new birth God's Spirit brings life to our spirit and lives within us to restore to us once again the

27

knowledge of God our Father. Yet we conclude that the "roller coaster ride" is still inevitable, due to our own stubbornness! We not want to give up control of our intellect, will and emotions (which have governed us for years) to our new baby spirit.

So now we are born again of the Spirit, yet we live in the soul. As Watchman Nee expresses it,

> Christians often account what is soulical as spiritual, and thus they remain in a soulish state and seek not what is really spiritual. How can we escape loss if we confuse what God has divided? Spiritual knowledge is very important to spiritual life.[1]

We must come to God's Word, which is "living and active. Sharper than any double-edged sword, it penetrates even to dividing soul and spirit, joints and marrow; it judges the thoughts and attitudes of the heart" (Heb. 4:12, NIV).

When I received the Lord Jesus I was born again; my spirit passed from death to new life in Christ. I am now on a journey of daily, progressive change, from glory to glory being changed by Him.

> Praise be to the God and Father of our Lord Jesus Christ! In his great mercy he has given us new birth into a living hope through the

---

[1] Watchman Nee, *Spiritual Man*, Vol. 1, p. 22

resurrection of Jesus Christ from the dead [spiritually], and into an inheritance that can never perish, spoil or fade—kept in heaven for you, who through faith are shielded by God's power until the coming of the salvation that is ready to be revealed in the last time. In this you greatly rejoice, though now for a little while you may have had to suffer grief in all kinds of trials. These have come so that your faith—of greater worth than gold, which perishes even though refined by fire—may be proved genuine and may result in praise, glory and honor when Jesus Christ is revealed. Though you have not seen him, you love him; and even though you do not see him now, you believe in him and are filled with an inexpressible and glorious joy, for you are receiving the goal of your faith, the salvation of your souls. (1 Pet. 1:3-9, NIV)

The salvation of my soul is said to be the goal of my faith. The spirit is born again and made alive, new. My soul is now that which needs salvation. I need to come to realize that a great struggle for survival is going on within me. My soul does not want to die or lose control to another. Herein lies my problem.

Now this is no great new discovery; we've heard it proclaimed over and over. We know there is a battle ever waging within us. So what's new? Only the way we choose to understand and view the struggle.

Peter puts it like this:

In this you greatly rejoice, [our salvation and inheritance] though now for a little while you may have had to suffer grief in all kinds of trials. (1 Pet. 1:6, NIV)

How do you view the "all kinds of trials"? Each day of my life I expect circumstances to come into my life, trials and tribulations which force me to learn and which reveal my hidden attitudes. These trials and testings are intended to improve my walk, so that I may in turn help others. The Lord is there to examine my attitude and the intent of my heart. I can now either help or harm others in their walk. We discovered how the Israelites viewed trials. They murmured and complained. They accused God of wanting to kill them. What is our parallel position? We murmur and complain. We accuse God of wanting to kill us, or at least of not loving us.

Peter said it was these very trials that would produce the faith (the "tried and fried" faith) that would bring us to our goal—the "salvation of our soul."

We, like the Israelites, look at our situation and

then judge God. Oh, we would not admit to judging God. Just like the Israelites, we blame the other person involved in the situation. Let's look and see:

> In the desert the whole community *grumbled against Moses and Aaron.* The Israelites said to them, "If only we had died by the Lord's hand in Egypt! There we sat around pots of meat and ate all the food we wanted, but you have brought us out into this desert to starve this entire assembly to death." (Exod. 16:2, 3 NIV, italics mine)

Then the Lord said to Moses,

> I will rain down bread from heaven for you. The people are to go out each day and gather enough for that day. In this way I will *test* them and see whether they will follow my instructions. (Exod. 16:4 NIV, italics mine)

> Isn't it amazing how we don't want the test, just the bread?

> On the sixth day they are to prepare what they bring in, and that is to be twice as much as they gather on the other days. (Exod. 16:5, NIV)

31

Would you believe there were some out there on the seventh day to gather? They failed the test God gave them to see if they could hear Him at all or still only hear self.

So Moses and Aaron said to all the Israelites,

In the evening you will know [when you eat the meat of the quail] that it was the Lord who brought you out of Egypt, [not just Moses and Aaron] and in the morning you will see the glory of the Lord [the bread from heaven that covered the ground, taking care of their physical needs], because *he has heard your grumbling against him.* Who are we [Moses and Aaron], that you should grumble against us? . . . You are not grumbling against us, but against the Lord. (Exod. 16:6-8 NIV, italics mine)

In our own surroundings we might have a situation where we are found grumbling. Maybe it's an unsaved husband. "If only he were saved, my whole life would be different. My husband won't let me mention the Lord. He just can't make the right decisions. He won't discipline the kids. He makes me do it all." Does this sound like your position? How do you handle this situation?

Negativity sets you back in your walk. This

may be a trial for patience, for forgiveness, or possibly for your liberty from negative thinking toward your circumstances.

You might have an unkind, unsympathetic mother-in-law. Unkind sister-in-law? A boss who doesn't see your potential, who always gives you the underdog position, who treats you like dirt, like you don't have a brain, etc.? We all have someone in our life who creates situations that cause us grief and pain. Do we just sit in the situation, have a pity party, become hardened and unfeeling, develop a chip-on-the-shoulder, and become unreachable and untouchable? What attitudes do we form inside? These will determine whether we have bondage to self or liberation from our soul—that is, from our *emotions*, thoughts ("Judges the thoughts and attitudes of the heart"— Heb. 4:12), and volition. How will I choose to respond to my situation and to the people involved?

If I choose to see the hand of God at work for the salvation of my soul, I will come to liberty. If I choose to murmur and complain about my situation—about how uniquely different my situation is—then I am stuck in bondage to my soul and self, not realizing I am complaining against God, who gave me the test. I am being tested! God is seeing if I can hear him through my newborn spirit. I am being brought to the death of self-control and into the control of the Holy Spirit.

Those who lie according to the sinful [soulish] nature have their *minds* set on what that nature desires; but those who live in accordance with the Spirit have their minds set on what the Spirit desires (Rom. 8:5 NIV, italics mine)

This, then, is our problem and our struggle defined: Where to from here?

A young lady came to see me recently and expressed her failure to overcome certain habits, desires and "want tos" in her life.

"I still want to party and be a part of my friends," she said. Her friends still used drugs and marijuana to reach the state which they think "partying" is all about. "I still want to disco. What's wrong with my having fun my way?"

Her struggle was getting so intense that she didn't want to be around people—especially those in her church group. She was sick of their demands, and she was unable to meet their *expectations* of her. Pointed to God's Word, she had been shown that the Lord God expects a change, both in our friendships and in what we used to do for fun (1 Pet. 4:2, 3). We then talked about expectations in marriage, how that the husband has certain expectations of a wife. Just as the husband is the head of the wife, Christ is the head of the Church. A God-fearing wife (that is, one who has an awesome wonder of His person) desires to meet her husband's expectations and does not expect him to bend and give in to hers. So it is with our relationship with the Lord.

She did not agree with meeting His desires instead of His giving in to hers. It simply brought her frustration to the surface. She asked, "Don't you have expectations? I expect certain things from the Lord, and He lets me down."

Now what were her expectations? The same as today's "modern" bride, who tells her husband, "I expect certain freedoms—no submitting—no obeying—fifty-fifty on duties—if I don't feel like cleaning the house don't expect it of me; I expect you to understand my feelings of not wanting always to bend to your demands—after all, I am a person with my own rights to be considered, too! No picking up dirty socks and skivvies, no waiting on you and meeting your desires; remember, I desire too. There are certain things I just plain and simply do not want to be bothered with. However, I expect *you* to be loving, kind and gentle, to treat me always with your giving love, and to do for me all those things which I cannot and do not want to do for you."

Now I have exaggerated this scene a little to get your attention. Jesus is coming to claim His bride. What kind of bride are you telling him you are choosing to be like?

"Jesus, I love you, *but* I expect you to understand my weaknesses, and please do not expect too much of me. You know I'm sick; I just can't do certain things. You know I'm weak; I just can't choose to stop this thing (whatever it is that keeps me in bondage to the self-will and flesh). I expect that you will please just not expect me to change for you. Just accept me like I am! I don't want to let go of myself to conform to your expectations of me. I do not want to let go of my anger or resentment toward my husband. He is the one who needs to change (or apply that to your child, wife, boss, teacher, pastor, or anyone else). I cannot forgive what was done or said to me. The hurt is too deep. It's too hard for me— don't you understand?"

One day my husband, Dennis, asked me to paint under the eaves of our house. To reach the eaves I needed to climb a ladder. Our ladder was old, and it had no place to set the paint bucket, so I would have to hold the bucket in one hand and the brush in the other, and then balance myself on this not-very-stable ladder. My husband had an expectation. I had a problem. I could not take heights; they petrified me. Now I truly wanted to fulfill his expectations, I tried and tried, prayed and prayed some more, but I could not do what my husband asked. To him it was such a simple task. Now he became upset with me, and I got mad at him. (I expected him to understand and then not expect of me what I couldn't do. Oh, how I was frustrated!) Now I mentioned a prayer for help. I expected, of all things, that the Lord would understand and then take care of my husband (but good) for expecting such a thing from his poor, little, defenseless wife. (Ha!)

We needed the eaves painted, because we were moving. Our new house was a two-story home, with a staircase that (to me) went to heaven and back. Was the Lord going to help me off the ladder? No, he gave me a higher ladder (the staircase) to climb. The Lord had expectations too. He knew that in Him I was complete and could do all things, so He just expected me to do what was required. I could do one of two things: "trust and obey," or fume, murmur, rebel, sit tight, clench my teeth, kick my heels, and say, "I can't, you are mean, cruel and unjust, and you're just expecting too much of me!" Get the point?

My spirit lifts to the Lord to hear, worship, adore, and love Him. My soul says, "You love *Me*, give to *Me*, do for *Me*. Please understand and don't expect." Jesus desires that my soul (my intellect, emotions and will) increase in faith to realize what I can't do and really don't feel much like doing. I can choose to know that I can *if I really want to*. It is my choice (He can't choose for me) to reach the goal of my faith—the salvation of my soul. Through His testings and trials—like learning to climb because He has expectations of me—we can then discern the thoughts, attitudes (like self-pity?) and intentions of our heart.

The choice I have to make in my testing (like with the ladder and Dennis's expectations) involves my heart motive. Do I demand that he bend to my expectations or give in to my fears and feelings? ("You know I can't climb that ladder; don't expect me to.") The choice also concerns the attitude I form from that test. The easiest attitude to form is self-pity. From self-pity comes pouting and then the intentional hardening of the heart not to budge.

The Lord has a different expectation. He desires death to self and death to self-indulgence. I indulge myself (my soul) when I give in to the attitude I am forming. Then the intention of my heart is to feel sorry for myself and my fear of heights. To indulge myself is to lick my wounds and center in on my fear. My fear becomes my excuse and my "security blanket." I can nurture and indulge that fear, or I can face the test as from my Heavenly Father, who wants me to be victorious, to overcome my fear, and to come to the salvation of my soul. He does not want me to indulge my fear.

At this point, some of us would become

sympathetic and understanding and help the person off the ladder. We would console them, letting them know the fear is real, that it's for self-protection. "Don't force yourself; just hang in there."

The salvation of my soul would be my liberation from fear. God's infinite mercy and wisdom are above my thoughts and wisdom. He gives me heights higher than the ladder I could not climb for my husband. His (the Lord's) expectation for me was to face the fear, walk into it and be free, and be liberated. His desire was for me to experience my salvation through the test. My faith was in His great love to see me through what my mind was telling my emotions was impossible for me to accomplish. By obedience to the Lord's expectations of me (you can do it, you know), my choice was to let go of the fear that said no and commit that fear to Him. We climbed. (I can now climb a ladder all the way to the top of our roof.)

The tests are my Father's choice for me, because He knows just how much I can do. My choice is to trust and obey (sometimes the frustration and anger take awhile to subside before I can obey without self-pity) and come to the goal of my faith—the salvation of my soul. Then I will not have the self-control which keeps me bound, but the Spirit-control which leads to liberty.

I can hear some of you saying, "Easier said than

done." You're right. He doesn't guarantee us an easy road, but He does guarantee a road to liberty in Him! He promised, He walked the road first, and He learned all we need to know to make it. It is because He walked it first that He has such great expectations for us. He doesn't let us down (as my young friend felt); He just refuses to listen to our limited view. He's coming from an expanded, victorious viewpoint. In fact, He said,

> I have told you these things, so that in me you may have peace. In this world you will have trouble. But take heart! I have overcome the world. (John 16:33 NIV)

4

Submit: Who, Me?

When I speak of liberty from bondage, I refer strictly to those inner attitudes and passive ways that keep us bound to self-indulgences. I am not teaching liberation from our God-given roles as helpmates (Gen. 2 and 3).

Before you think I am going to step on some toes, let me assure you that I know that some women do need to work outside the home. I realize that in that case husbands do need to help at home. I am really concerned only with the attitude of self-pity, which feels sorry for "poor little me," which says, "No one loves and cares for me." I believe very much that when you have to work outside the home—to take care of financial hardships and not just to support a life style beyond your means—your husband still carries the headship role.

In Genesis 2 and 3, God put a special order to things after the fall. I believe that Eve had special rights of equality before she "blew it" (Gen. 3:1-6).

When she disobeyed by following her own volition, she got into trouble. Because God had created humankind, He made the necessary decisions that followed their downfall. To the women He said, "I will greatly increase your pain in childbearing; with pain you will give birth to children." Now God, knowing how we would react by staying away from our men, continued, "Your desire will be for your husband." God put inside us a desire and craving for our husbands: "and he (your husband) will rule over you."

It is against that "rule over you" that we constantly rebel. Actually, we are rebelling against God, who put it into effect.

Now I am addressing you Christian wives who believe in and rely on the Lord Jesus as Lord of your lives and who stand on His promises. Around us today is staggering, overwhelming, growing divorce rate—not only in the world, but in the Church. I'm sure you've noticed.

Recently to combat this problem, many churches formed classes for women. These classes used a certain book, which encouraged women to become seducers of their husbands. Some will recall the title right away; I will not even mention it, because I would not recommend it either to Christian wives or to group teaching sessions.

Seduction is not new. The Israelites got into trouble with that one too. As they journeyed into the Promised Land and claimed their inheritance, they were told to stay away from the customs and religious practices of the people around them. Again, they did not obey His Word. One practice was the worship of Asherah, "queen of heaven," consort to Baal. The women wove tapestries for tent hangings. The worship also included prostitution and sexual vices. All of this kindled God's wrath against the women and men of Israel. God declared that because of them and their seductive ways His name would be no more invoked in the mouth of any man of Judah (2 Kings 23:6, 7; Jer. 44:16-26). Would God stop calling the men and being part of their lives?

Years ago in my early Christian life I was part of a small church. On Sunday as the pews began to fill, I looked around and became aware that the women outnumbered the men. It was so very evident that the men were somewhere else and that in each pew were sad, lonely women. I began to seek God for the reasons. I even prayed one day, "Lord, if heaven is going to be filled with only women, I really don't want to be there." Over the years those Scriptures—2 Kings 23:6, 7 and Jeremiah 44:21—came into focus. Was it possible that women were trying to seduce their husbands into the Kingdom? Was there in women a subtle form of seduction, called manipulation? The church was teaching women who had unsaved husbands, "Woman, you are a believer; your husband is not. You take the spiritual headship and get the family to church on Sunday and midweek. You need the prayer and Bible study." A form of Sunday manipulation followed. "Set the example—be the lead." Husbands began to disappear.

What happened to 1 Peter 3:1? "In like manner you married women, be submissive to your own husbands. . ." (TAB). We were taught, "If he doesn't come to church with you, you take the kids and go yourselves." The Amplified Bible continues in 1 Peter 3:1 with "subordinate yourselves as being secondary to and dependent on them, and adapt yourselves to them [husbands]."

"Even if my husband wants me to stay home on Sunday?"

First Peter 3:1: "So that even if any do not obey the Word [of God], they may be won over not by discussion but by the [godly] lives of their wives" (TAB).

It seems we women forget that God desires our men to become believers more than we do. Isn't He capable of drawing them, wooing them, winning them? Doesn't God want men in heaven? God placed our husbands to be head over us, not only if they are Christian husbands. Peter says to be dependent on them and adapt to them. The husband is not to adapt himself to the wife. If he is not obeying God's Word he can be won by the godly life of the wife. The godly life is that of submission, respect, and reliance on the husband— not that of usurping authority and taking on headship in spiritual matters. That leads to independence and taking the control in other areas in question as well.

Seduction, manipulation and vices are not going to unite a home or bring a husband into a relationship with the Lord Jesus as Savior. God placed our husbands over us to be our headship and authority. We don't need to seduce them or use sex to gain control over them in order to get our own way.

God will not woo them to himself or speak to them through His Word if we continue to stand between the two.

We've already talked about expectations, but let's look at them again. Is it only a husband who should have his expectations met? Shouldn't we as wives have any expectations at all? Again I refer to our Bible as a guide to Christian wives for role models.

First Peter 3:1-6 (TAB):

> In like manner you married women, be submissive to your own husbands—subordinate yourselves as being secondary to and dependent on them.

45

(Did I lose any of you yet? We've only just begun.)

> *And adapt yourselves to them.* So that even if any do not obey the Word [of God], they may be won over not by discussion (italics mine).

(You don't really have to beat them over the head with the Bible.)

> But by the [godly] lives of their wives,

(Actions speak louder than words always.)

> When they observe the pure

(Heart attitude.)

> And modest way in which you conduct yourselves, together with your reverence [for your husband. That is, you are to feel for him all that reverence includes]— to respect,

(That's a toughy when their behavior isn't one we want to respect.)

> Defer to, revere him; [revere means] to honor, esteem (appreciate, prize), and [in the human sense] adore him; [and adore means] to admire, praise, be devoted to, deeply love and enjoy [your husband].

Let not yours be the [merely] external
adorning with [elaborate] interweaving and
knotting of the hair, the wearing of jewelry,
or changes of clothes;
But let it be the *inward* adorning and beauty
of the hidden person. (italics mine)

(Heart attitude.)

of the heart, with the incorruptible and
unfading

(Doesn't change with every little whim.)

charm of a gentle

(No shrew.)

and peaceful spirit, which (is not anxious
or wrought up, but) is very precious in
the sight of God. . . .
It was thus that Sarah obeyed Abraham
(following his guidance and acknowledging his headship over her by) calling him
lord. . . .

How, actually, did Sarah obey and respect, love
and adore Abraham (Gen. 12 and 20)? Abraham
led his family from his father's land. See what
attitude you might form. Your husband comes

home one night after a hard day at the office. . . .

"Hon, I'm home, start packing."

"Where are we going?"

"Oh, I don't know."

"How long will we be gone?"

"Probably the rest of our lives."

How would you react to leaving your family and friends of a lifetime to follow your husband to a land you know nothing about? How would you respond to the thought of leaving a cozy home and fireplace to wander from that time on in tents and become nomads? Would your heart attitude remain pure in respect? Would you still defer to, revere, honor and esteem your husband?

As Abraham and Sarah (or Abram and Sarai, as they were called at first) journeyed, a famine took them to Egypt, where there was food. Now Abraham looked at Sarah, who was beautiful, and said, "Say you are my sister, so that I will be treated well for your sake and my life will be spared because of you" (Gen. 12:13 NIV).

He wanted his neck to be spared, but he let his wife be taken into the Pharaoh's harem. How would you be feeling about that? ("Some man I've got! He wants me to be sent into some guy's harem just to save his own life. What about me? What happens to me? My own husband won't stand up and defend himself or me. What is he, a coward?") Where does the heart attitude of respect, deference, reverence, honor and esteem go now? What attitude would you have?

That didn't happen just once in Sarah's life— you got it, it happened again. This time Abraham was hitting 100 years old, and Sarah ninety-nine, and God had just promised them a child who would carry on the covenant promise of God.

Again, Abraham and Sarah were on a journey. This time they were temporary residents around Gerar.

> Abraham said of his wife Sarah, "She is my sister." Then Abimelech . . . took her [into his harem]. (Gen. 20:2 NIV)

How do we see Sarah both times? I see her as having an abiding inner quiet and peace. She did not react in an overanxious tizzy. She was not in a rage of temper, resolving never to speak to him again. She did not whip him down with a barrage of words about cruel and unjust treatment, nor did she run to the nearest lawyer and file for divorce.

She was not alone in her situation, nor was she destitute or abandoned. She had all the help she needed because her heart attitude remained pure. No hatred, resentment or anger were in her.

In Genesis 12:16, Abraham was paid sheep, oxen, he-donkeys, maidservants, she-donkeys, and camels for Sarah.

> *But the Lord* inflicted serious diseases on Pharaoh. (Gen. 12:17 NIV)

(Not on Abraham; most of us would want God to scourge our husbands for treating us like that and getting away with it.)

> And his household because of Abram's wife Sarai. (Gen. 12:17 NIV)

Again, in Genesis 20:3,

> *But God* came to Abimelech in a dream one night and said to him, "You are as good as dead because of the woman you have taken; she is a married woman."

The beauty in Sarah was the peace of knowing that God was God and that He was the head over her husband, who was the head over her. When Abraham made the wrong choices and made big blunders, she, his wife, did not have to correct him or change him. The wife still had God's faithful hand upon her man. Our only problem in not seeing the reality of this today is our independent spirit. We neither become totally dependent upon our husbands nor upon God. Now we depend upon our education, training and ability to take care of ourselves and make good, sound judgments on our own.

We know as wives that if our husbands were to sell us to a harem we could reason things out logically and show our husbands that they're crazy if they think we will go along with such a stupid thing. Then we could: (1) get a divorce; (2) get a good paying job; (3) collect alimony; and (4) be free.

Think of what Sarah would have missed. By being totally dependent on her man and on the Lord God, she reaped the benefits of seeing God's hand move.

We women of today have education and independence; we can decide for ourselves what we want and when we want it. We can be free from pressure, hassles, hardships, and temperamental husbands. We can dream and fantasize about the man we should have married—the husband who would never lose his temper, never ask too much, not be demanding or unreasonable, never strike out in anger, never become a drunk, gambler or nonprovider. I'm sure you're adding your own list.

We can sit before the Lord and moan and cry about how we made a mistake, how we just didn't get the right husband. Sarah certainly could have said that! Again I direct our attention to our inner attitudes. Sarah kept a pure heart attitude that did not tie God's hands. He was free to move in on both situations and free Sarah. He freed her to be joined right back to Abraham. God did not free her to pity herself or release her from her husband because he had made the wrong decision.

When Sarah was given back to Abraham there was within her an ever-remaining beauty that shone outward. (What king would want a ninety-nine-year-old woman in his harem? What did he see that Abraham saw?) I believe that because of her submissive heart and forgiving attitude, God renewed her youth (Ps. 103:5). As we praise the Lord and trust Him, our attitudes change the age lines of anger on our faces.

We are told that the eyes are the mirrors of our heart. Sarah's eyes must have reflected the inner peace and the adoration she had for Abraham even when he was wrong. That is the beauty expressed in 1 Peter 3:1-6. We can look in the faces of today, with all their eyeshadow, liner, braids and elaborate paint jobs, and still see hard eyes. A paint job on the outside can't camouflage what is really there inside—the real you, expressing the true feelings.

God has set husbands over us to be our covering and rule, only because He sees the need for it in our lives. All men do not understand how to take that place of leadership. Not all women want their men to have that place in their lives.

We need to come to a heart agreement with God's order. It was God's plan; He didn't plan it incorrectly. The only problem is that Satan is still around fouling up your Garden of Eden (home, marriage, and family). Satan does not want the home to be happy or God's plan to be fulfilled.

The Israelites were plagued with Asheroth worship and seduction. Satan is still coming at us through TV and movies, billboards and commercials. The "im-morals" of the world are displayed before us. If you're not happy with Jim, find a John. Jim can find Sally. If Sally finds no happiness, she can turn Jim in for Pete.

Self-love, self-gratification, and self-indulgence are still the center core to be worked with. Self has to be dethroned. Without the death of self we are never free from the self-demands of each other. These demands are placed on each other so that individuals' selfish wills can maintain control. When death comes to self, marriage becomes what God planned it to be. His purpose is fulfilled, and we can see His mighty hand released to move upon our hearts and homes.

God's plan has not changed. Our men are to rule over us. When our heart attitudes can agree that God is right, we can submit to His plan, and things can change.

We need to develop a heart attitude of

dependence upon our husbands and upon our Lord Jesus Christ. There comes a time to relinquish our stubborn independence. Jesus is head of the Church, as the husband is the head of the wife. We are to: "Be subject—be submissive and adapt yourselves—to your own husbands as [a service] to the Lord" (Eph. 5:22, TAB).

One quick note on submission: submission does not mean becoming a doormat to be used and stepped upon. Submission is having and keeping a heart attitude that is teachable, bendable, docile, pliant and tame.

Webster's dictionary defines "submissive" as: "willing or inclined to submit; to give to another; yield to authority, surrender. To present for the judgment or decision of another."

"Docile," on the other hand, is defined as: "Amenable to training, easy to manage. Synonyms: amenable, compliant, gentle, manageable, *obedient*, pliant, pliable, submissive, tame, teachable, tractable, yielding."

One who is *docile* is easily taught. One who is *tractable* is easily led.

One who is *pliant* is easily bent in any direction. *Compliant* represents one as inclined or persuaded to agreement with another's will. The following are antonyms for docile: determined, dogged, firm, inflexible, intractable, obstinate, opinionated, resolute, self-willed, stubborn, unyielding, willful.

We are not to be stubborn, unteachable, dogmatic, firm, unbendable. We can submit how we feel about certain issues. We may express our opinion and "put in our two cents worth," but it is submitted to a higher authority for his final decision. All of this is hard for us as human beings because of the "tree of the knowledge of good and evil," or rights and wrongs. We as individuals—and this has nothing to do with man and wife—like to be right, and it kills us to be considered wrong. Do you see why self has to be crucified?

Submissiveness means I can have my own views and opinions, that I can speak up, but that my husband has the last word on the subject. I fit in. If I know he is wrong and I am right, my heart attitude must remain pure toward him. I can then talk to the Head over my head and submit how I feel to Him. Then the whole responsibility is with God, and not with me.

So it is still our heart attitude that we check and double-check, so that the inner beauty of a peaceful woman can be seen by our men. It is amazing what dripping honey instead of vinegar can do for the disposition of a husband. A prayerful heart and a total trust in Jesus are that source of inner peace.

Let's take time to read. Proverbs 31:10-31 is a description of the kind of wife one mother told her son to look for. She would be rare and almost impossible to find, but when he did find her she would be a priceless wife.

A wife of noble character who can find? She is worth far more than rubies. Her husband has full confidence in her and lacks nothing of value. She brings him good [selfless living], not harm, all the days of her life.
She selects wool and flax and works with eager hands.
She is like the merchant ships, bringing her food from afar.
She gets up while it is still dark; she provides food for her family and portions for her servant girls.
She considers a field and buys it; out of her earnings she plants a vineyard.

(This wife not only keeps up her own house and duties, but also holds a productive job outside. She doesn't come in tired out after work and sit down and expect her husband to pamper her.)

She sets about her work vigorously; her arms are strong for her tasks.
She sees that her trading is profitable, and her lamp does not go out at night. In her hand she holds the distaff and grasps the spindle with her fingers.

(She not only made the clothes, but also wove the material.)

She opens her arms to the poor and extends her hands to the needy.
When it snows, she has no fear for her household; for all of them are clothed in scarlet.
She makes coverings for her bed; she is clothed in fine linen and purple.
Her husband is respected at the city gate, where he takes his seat among the elders of the land.
She makes linen garments and sells them, and supplies the merchants with sashes.

(It doesn't sound like she has idle time to sit in a coffee klatch sharing the latest tidbits of gossip—or to sit in front of the "boob tube" watching the latest soap opera.)

Strength and dignity are her clothing, and she smiles at the future.
She opens her mouth in wisdom, And the teaching of kindness is on her tongue.
She looks well to the ways of her household, And does not eat the bread of idleness.
Her children rise up and bless her; Her husband also, and he praises her, saying:

"Many daughters have done nobly, But you excel them all."
Charm is deceitful and beauty is vain, But a woman who fears the Lord, she shall be praised. Give her the product of her hands, And let her works praise her in the gates. (Prov. 31:25-31 NASB)

The description of this wife in Proverbs is to me the description also of the Bride Jesus would desire and that the Father would desire for Him. Most of us agree that we would surely be that kind of wife if our husbands were like Jesus. Maybe the husbands would become more like Jesus quicker if there were more selfless, unselfish wives tending to the family needs as helpmates should.

Seduction, or manipulation, is not God's order. Marriage is hard work, submissiveness, and obedience. Liberty results when the right ingredients are forming an ongoing, right heart attitude. Bondage results when self-love and self-indulgence demand their fulfillment. Don't let soap operas and Hollywood make you become a seductress. Become the woman God wants; then He is free to move upon the head who is over you. God desires the right order—He wrote it out. Our bondage and drudgeries come when we go against His perfect plan and choose the world's humanistic,

Satan-oriented plans. Satan's plan is destruction and separation of marriage partners. God's view is:

> I hate divorce and marital separation, and him who covers his garment [his wife] with violence. Therefore, keep a watch upon your spirit [that it may be controlled by My Spirit], that you deal not treacherously and faithlessly [with your marriage mate]. (Mal. 2:16, TAB)

The Lord God hates divorce and separation. Many of our homes are feeling the effects of marriage partners who are living together but who have become separated in their hearts because of bitterness, anger, hatred, jealousy, envy, and strife. All these sins against God and against each other need our daily prayers for forgiveness, and as Malachi stated, we need to be controlled by God's Holy Spirit so that we do not fulfill our lusts (anger, rage, hostility, etc.).

In Galatians 5:16 we read,

> But I say, walk and live habitually in the (Holy) Spirit—responsive to and controlled and guided by the Spirit; then you will certainly not gratify the cravings and desires of the flesh—of human nature without God.

Together, husband and wife are one whole person. Instead of criticizing and putting each other down for the weaknesses in your lives, learn to become the strength the other needs.

My husband is a saver of money; I am a spender. When we were first married, money was a major cause for our arguments. I did not want my weakness covered by his strength. I thought I needed certain things to be fulfilled in order to run the home, care for the kids, and be satisfied. My husband had projected his thoughts toward the future, and he saved. Every pay increase went into savings, and only a small percentage of the raise came home. I lived for right now and the needs of right now. My husband did not give into my weakness, nor did he let me indulge my weakness. Because he stayed strong, I too (after many frustrating years) became a part of his strength, and we became one in the area of money management. Today I see through his eyes. The years it took to get to the oneness were not without problems, believe me—we had them. Dennis was very critical and at times harsh. I thought he was worse than Scrooge. Because we love each other and the Lord, however, we made it through. It would not have taken so long had we known what we know now.

Don't just put each other down for a weakness. Don't just walk off in disgust and assume neither one can change or assume that's the way they are and always will be. Jesus requires a change in our behavior. In patience and love toward each other we can edify and build each other up in love.

Jesus told Paul, "My grace is sufficient for thee: for my strength is made perfect in weakness" (2 Cor. 12:9 KJV). He would actually become the strength for our weaknesses. (What things are you weak in; have you ever listed them on paper?) If I am bound by fears, He will be my strength away from, or through, those fears.

It was to have been the same in marriage. I say, "was to have been," because so many partners give up on each other when they see the other's weaknesses. The Scriptures imply that everyone has faults, or weaknesses (see Ps. 19:12; James 5:16). For example, Paul speaks of his "thorn in the flesh" in 2 Cor. 12, for which Jesus' grace was to be sufficient. Now some of us have decidedly more than one, some more than fifteen. Some don't like to admit to any, but just ask their mates—you'll find them out!

So we have weaknesses. Now what? In the same way that Jesus promised to become our strength, we have to become strengths for each other. When my fear of heights gets in the way, my husband's strength can be my salvation from fear.

In some situations, when a wife has a fear it is

greeted by a husband's scorn and contempt. In such a situation, needless to say, the husband has not become the strength his wife needs to overcome the fear but has only, through his destructive attitudes, reinforced the fear. What the wife needs is the strength of the husband to overcome. Then the two are one in strength and unity of mind.

The bondage to criticism and condemnation of others is usually incited by the weaknesses we cannot face in our own lives, so we seem compelled to lash out at others. This does not help either person overcome weaknesses but keeps both in bondage.

Again, the path to liberty is in honesty. You will never be free from weaknesses in your lifetime. I have them, and so do you. We do have to be honest with ourselves and with others, and admit to our weaknesses.

As a husband and wife it is good to sit down together (letting the Holy Spirit guide you) and write a list of strengths and weaknesses. Compare and talk about the lists, then become the strength for each other's weaknesses and become one whole person.

1. What are your fears? Write them down.

2. Do you realize what fear is?

Sit down together without suggesting what your mate's weaknesses are. Concentrate on your own. With some, this will be difficult. We sometimes push our own faults out of our conscious range. Ask the Holy Spirit to reveal your weaknesses. Then be truthful and honest with your evaluation. (See Ps. 51:6.)

5

The Bondages That Are Still With Us

Stand fast therefore in the liberty wherewith Christ hath made us free, and be not
entangled again with the yoke of bondage.
(Gal. 5:1 KJV)

We have followed the Israelites out of bondage
to the Egyptians and have seen them safely
through the Red (Reed) Sea. The Lord God
guided them by a cloud by day and a fiery cloud
(Exod. 13:21) by night. They were on their
journey with the Lord showing them the way.
Their focus was on that cloud of God's presence.
When the cloud stopped, they stopped and camped
until it moved again. The Israelites were led daily
on their journey to the Promised Land. What a joy
they expressed as the Sea closed behind them,
destroying their enemy:

I will sing to the Lord, for He has triumphed
gloriously. (Exod. 15:1, TAB)

Don't you feel like that; or should I say, didn't you feel just like that when you met Jesus and started your journey with Him? The enemy seemed to have been annihilated, and life was so gloriously new and wonderful! We sang:

> The Lord is my strength and my song, and He has become my salvation; this is my God, and I will praise Him, my father's God, and I will exalt Him. . .
> Your right hand, O Lord, is glorious in power; Your right hand, O Lord, shatters the enemy. (Exod. 15:2, 6, TAB)

Our relationship with the Lord seemed so strong that nothing could cause our joy or trust to fade. That seemed to be the heart attitude of all Israel as they began their journey.

Moses continued to lead his little flock, and they journeyed for three days in the wilderness of Shur. This desert was hot, and the people became tired after walking around in it. They began to come down from their glorious high of a few days before. Their body senses began to speak up and be heard. Their eyes began to see and take notice of a vast and barren wasteland. Soon these impressions were transmitted to the mind, which in turn relayed to the saliva glands messages which said, "Hey, I'm thirsty! You know, a guy could die out here with no water, and from the looks of things all around me there is no way to get water."

Now the cloud of God's presence was leading the people onward. In three days of walking did not God know they would be thirsty? He created our bodies; does He not know a body cannot survive beyond three days without water? Was He trying to tell them something, something that He knew so well they would not pay attention to?

In 430 years of captivity they knew of their God, but they did not serve Him. They had lived a life of servitude to Pharaoh, doing as he dictated, fulfilling his every wish and desire. They were in total bondage, not free to choose to do as they pleased. They were told when to rise, work, rest, eat and sleep. All was done according to Pharaoh's commands.

Now the Lord was bringing them away from the place of severe servitude and under His own leadership. They were to learn a new life style. They were free from bondage (from being told continuously what to do and when to do it) and from slavery. They were now going to experience the fact that as a free people they could not take careless advantage of their freedoms. They had to develop a new sense of hearing and obeying.

Each of us has lived a life as a captive and a slave. Oh, not to a Pharaoh, but to the self that ruled over us. Self dictates when to rise, work, rest, eat and sleep. Pharaoh had desires, wishes and choices which the slaves had to fulfill. Self has appetites, desires, cravings, wishes and choices that demand to be fulfilled. Self rules. Self goes by feelings—feelings which gratify, fulfill and please the individual. When we receive Christ as our divine authority and ruler of our lives, we too have to begin the daily process of changing whom it is we listen to and obey. We now need to choose to fulfill God's heart for us and to hear His desires, wishes and choices—not our own. Self speaks so loud at times that we cannot hear God's directions or wishes for us.

So on the third day of the Israelites' journey, God knew they would be thirsty. He tested the area that needed testing. To thirst is not bad. To need water is not bad. The Lord was trying to let them know that they were still thinking like slaves, even though He had just made them a free people. Thirst is an eager desire. Sometimes the desires of our flesh are so strong that we simply feel, "I'll just die if they're not gratified immediately."

We can thirst for knowledge and wisdom, and soon wisdom becomes our "god." If others do not show forth the same scope of wisdom, we tear them down. In our mind they are worth nothing. We can thirst for power and want to rule and use people. We can thirst for wealth, love, friendship, or a mate. None of these things are wrong until the thing we thirst for becomes our idol, and we worship the thing instead of our God. None of these things are wrong until we hurt and abuse people just to achieve our own eager desires.

Thirst (eager desire) was the first area uncovered on the journey. (By the way, God didn't let them die of thirst—He gave them water to drink. And He revealed the bitterness in their hearts.) They had not traveled too far before their stomachs started to growl. Hunger was a real situation. Again, I believe that since God is the Creator He knew they would get hungry, but that He waited to give them food because He was testing another area. To hunger is to have a longing, a craving— any strong desire. Hunger, like thirst, is not bad if it is not the god of our lives. It is not bad if we are not in slavery on bondage to the appetites.

Synonyms for hunger include: appetency (instinct); craving, desire, disposition, impulse, inclination, liking, longing, lust, passion, proclivity (a natural disposition or tendency), proneness, propensity (same as proclivity), relish, thirst, zest, and Desire: to wish or long for the possession or enjoyment of; to covet, crave.

These are the areas the Father wants us to see and deal with. Who rules whom? We say Jesus is

Lord. But God knew the minute the Israelites followed Him that He was not regarded as the divine and only authority in their lives. When we receive Christ, He is not at first the only divine authority in our lives. The appetite is ruling.

What is it about appetite that rules? The very first synonym we listed is a good place to start. How's your instinct for survival? My instinct dictates, "I am a person of worth. I need recognition. I need to find myself and be fulfilled. Self does not want to let go and let God reign as King. A wife has problems being secondary to her husband. In groups it isn't easy to serve instead of being a leader. We fight to be seen, heard and recognized; we demand attention. Even those shrinking violets shrink to get recognition. Those who shy away are asking someone to come and pay attention. Each of us has his own ways of instinct. Mine are pretty strong. So were the Israelites' instincts for survival. Both times their cry was, "Have you brought us out here only to kill us with thirst and hunger?" (Exod. 15:24; 16:3). Self does not want to be dethroned; it wants to remain "god" of our lives. Self fights for survival, so the Lord has to come against it. God alone is to be obeyed.

David stood before Goliath and lay aside his instincts for personal survival. Those around him had begged him to put on Saul's armor (1 Sam. 17), but David could not walk because of its weight. The armor was self-protection, but he lay aside the instinct to protect self and went forth with total trust in God's care. Our instincts are always present, and we must, as David did, bring them under control.

Next in line were cravings. (Remember that each of these types of appetite is only wrong when it brings us under severe servitude.) The cravings in the mind, will and senses are numerous, as you will find out when you begin to name your own. Do they rule over you, or do you let the Holy Spirit control them? It is all well and good to have desires, until those desires take control.

Consider disposition. Do we have a disposition of selfish ambition that controls others or hurts others when they've hurt us? Or perhaps we have a disposition to hate, etc. Impulse, like instinct, causes immediate responses. We react on impulse to the influences of the world around us. We react on impulse to peer pressure, to husbands we fear, and to children who try to manipulate. Self indulgence is an obvious form of bondage to sensual cravings. Are we inclined to do whatever we feel like doing, whatever pleases self and gives us satisfaction and pleasure? Liking, longing, lust and passion: each can bring specific things to your mind.

God has given me much testing in these areas of self-preservation. For me, the specific thing was food. Food has been my biggest craving, desire, liking, longing, and lust. Eating was the way I stroked myself. When my husband sent hurtful things my way, when my children caused me pain, food was my solace. The feeling would arise within me that I was not appreciated: "I've worked so hard all day to get this house clean and what thanks do I get? None! He only saw what I didn't do." I'm sure you know the thoughts and feelings. They created a longing to be loved and appreciated, a proneness to self-pity, and then a trip to the refrigerator.

It wasn't really a matter of self-indulgence. My mind was too involved in replay to comprehend self-indulgence. The food was my comforter. Jesus wasn't; He couldn't make me feel appreciated. He would only remind me of selfless service to others, with love hardly even noticing the hurts others bring (1 Cor. 13). Who needs it? I didn't want a reminder of my own selfishness. I wanted God to see my family's selfishness and my virtuous servitude and perfection.

Needless to say, the Lord does know the truth about each of us, and because He is a good Father who dearly loves His children, He is bound to discipline us to deliver us from our self-centeredness and stubborn self-will. Thus we need to:

Stand fast therefore in the liberty wherewith
Christ hath made us free, and be not entangled
again with the yoke of bondage. (Gal. 5:1)

In our new life with Christ we must not misuse
our freedom from slavery. We want eternal life
and heaven guaranteed to us. But we live joyless,
defeated, faithless lives, merely because our Father
has begun to call attention to the gods we are
serving and following daily instead of Him.

He tests us only so that we can be honest and
truthful with Him. He only wants us to repent
from self-rule and learn to come under His divine
rule and authority. That is total liberty without
bondage. We need to be able to hear His still,
small voice over the roar of self-will. We are to
choose His will and good pleasure for our lives.
We don't seem to trust His will for our best
interest.

If I am to do God's will, I must know His will. To
know His will is to know His Word. I will fail only
when I do not know God's heart-felt communication with me. No amount of counseling will keep
me from falling if I am not grounded on the solid-
rock foundation. God's Word is the rock that
holds. It won't be all the church services I've
attended, or all the good books with all their
"how-tos" that I've read, that will help me stand
during my testings and trials. In order to under-

stand the "whys" and know what's going on, I must have an ever-deepening relationship with my new Lord and King. Then I will be able to hear and obey Him and dislodge the old ruler for the new (Matt. 7:24-27; Luke 6:46-49).

6

Are There Giants in Our Land?

When the Israelites finally reached their destination, ready to claim their promised inheritance (the land of Canaan), they discovered giants in their land. The Lord told them simply to go and possess the land.

He did not promise to eliminate the enemy in the land before they got there. He did promise that if they stepped forth and faced the enemy He would cause the enemy to be defeated.

The first spies sent in to look over their promised land came back to Moses to report on this beautiful place God had brought them to. Twelve spies were sent, one from each of the tribes of Israel. They all viewed the same scenes. Two have a positive view of the land; ten did not.

All twelve agreed on one thing:

We went into the land to which you sent us, and it does flow with milk and honey! Here is its fruit. (Num. 13:27 NIV)

This land was all the Lord had promised them it would be. The evidence was before their eyes. It was now just a matter of putting their feet into the land to walk through it and claim their inheritance.

For ten of the spies, possessing the land was a problem. They said,

> But the people who live there are powerful, and the cities are fortified and very large. (Num. 13:28 NIV)

> We can't attack those people; they are stronger than we are. (Num. 13:31 NIV)

Only Caleb and Joshua stood firm in their decision to go in:

> We should go up and take possession of the land, for we can certainly do it. (Num. 13:30)

> The land we passed through and explored is exceedingly good. If the Lord is pleased with us, he will lead us into that land, a land flowing with milk and honey, and will give it to us. Only do not rebel against the Lord. And do not be afraid of the people of the land, because we will swallow them up. Their protection is gone, but the Lord is with us. Do not be afraid of them. (Num. 14:7-9 NIV)

Are There Giants in Our Land?

By now you might be saying, "That's all well and good for them, but what does that have to do with me?" To them it was a real promise of a land to inherit if they would go forth with the Lord without rebellion or fear. We have their experience to look back on as an example and a warning not to grumble or rebel.

> These things happened to them as examples and were written down as warnings for us, on whom the fulfillment of the ages has come. (1 Cor. 10:11)

They were to possess the land. Let us make an analogy: let us picture our lives as a "land" to possess for the Lord. Now, do you have any "giants" in your land? The giants I refer to are those things in our lives that manifest themselves as nagging, frustrating, recurring problems that we cannot seem to break away from. These giants are our incriminating habits and attitudes. We can name them: bad temper or disposition, irritability, envy, hatred, malice. There are the anger and resentment that arise when others say or do things that bring me hurt. There is my inability to forgive others as Christ forgave me. The timidity that keeps me locked into myself. The inferiority complex that comes forth when I'm around certain people or when I'm called on to do certain things. My fear of failure. Guilt that overwhelms me when I fail, which makes it all seem so hopeless. These, along with many more, are the giants, the enemies that we must conquer in order to possess our land for the Lord.

Do I have "giants" in my life? We would all have to answer yes. Therefore the Lord gives us the same challenge today: go forth and possess your promised land—your total peace of mind and emotion. We started in Egypt, in slavery and captivity—our self-centered life without Christ. He heard our groanings and desired to set us free—free from our own self-bondages. His call to Israel (and to us), was,

> I am the Lord [redeemer, deliverer] and I will bring you out from under the yoke of the Egyptians [of self on the throne, ruling]. I will free you from being slaves to them, and will redeem you with an outstretched arm and with mighty acts of judgment. (Exod. 6:6 NIV)

Salvation was completed at the cross, but there is still a daily need for repentance, for forgiveness, and for laying down our lives for the sake of others. Accusations of Satan still need to be answered. He accuses us of our failures to be victorious believers. (Zech. 3:1-5; Job 1 and 2).

Like the Israelites, we need a Moses, not only to deliver us from bondage, but also to plead for us

and intercede for us because of the sins we
commit during our wilderness journey through
this life. Jesus is that person. He mediates and
intercedes before the Father in our behalf. He is
our High Priest who always hears our prayers
and the cries of our hearts. He prays constantly
for us that our faith will not fail (Luke 22:32). Our
temporary falls, which occur when the enemy is
not completely conquered, shall not condemn us,
for our High Priest ever intercedes for us.

The Israelites really did not want to leave Egypt,
for they like the customs and the food. What they
didn't like were the hard taskmasters. They
wanted Pharaoh eliminated and the hardships
ended while they continued their self-pleasures.
The Lord had to bring forth judgment upon the
land and the people around them to get them to
move and see things through different eyes.

So He desires us to come out of self and unto
Him (Exod. 6:7). He desires an intimate fellowship
with us, away from all that distracts and keeps us
from Him. We come out of captivity when we
come under the Lordship of Christ. We are
saying, "I renounce my right to rule my life
according to how I feel, think, or choose. I choose
you to rule in my place. You be my King. Thy
kingdom come on earth (my soul) as it is in
heaven."

We make that decision, and then we discover

that the giants in our lives do not agree with our letting Jesus be Lord, Ruler, and King. A lot of self-habits want to stay in high places in the mind and imagination. These are the giants in our land that stand between our soul and our Savior.

When Moses first stood before the land to lead the people to take possession, the Israelites rebelled. They would not be moved. Joshua cried out, "The Lord will give this land to us, only do not rebel against the Lord. And do not be afraid of the giants in the land." Well, at that point the people wanted to stone Joshua and Caleb to silence their voices. Isn't it amazing that just a few months ago God had shown them great and mighty miracles of His power? He had caused ten plagues upon the people and land of Egypt that caused Pharaoh to let the Israelites go from them as a free people. God had parted the Red Sea, given them manna and quail to eat, and guided them with a cloud by day and a fiery cloud by night. God was obviously and with great demonstration of power with them every step of the way. Now they had to make a choice on faith, believing He would continue to walk with them.

It's so easy for us to judge these people and say, "If I had been there I wouldn't have rebelled. I would have marched right in with Joshua and Caleb!" However, God has also asked us to possess a land for Him and conquer the giants.

We too have chosen just not to go in and conquer that temper, disposition, wrong reaction, or refusal to forgive, and have chosen just to sit in self-pity. The Lord's cry was, "How long will these people treat me with contempt? How long will they refuse to believe in me, in spite of all the miracles and signs I have performed among them?"

We look around us today and see evidence that a great many in the body of believers have not possessed the land—the self—for the Lord. They have received new life in Christ but still live in the old carnal nature. It's as if we believe Jesus for taking us all to heaven some day, but we just can't believe Him to help us in our daily walk. We still have to put up with the unsaved husband or wife and their obstinate temperaments. We fight the traffic, the boss, and the peer pressures. It seems this is all too much to believe that the Lord can handle. We have "up" days when we begin to see a glimmer of hope and a change in the behavior of those around us. Our faith has a surge of increase, only to be dashed because the day after the change in behavior, it became evident that there was really no change, and things went from bad to worse.

To a believer at those times, the joy fades and hope seems so very far away. That, in itself, is a giant of unbelief that the enemy wants to keep active in our lives. Satan is a liar and the father of lies. We need to recognize his lies as an enemy to conquer, instead of becoming defeated.

The Israelites were chastised by the Lord and caused to wander as strangers in the desert for forty years. After a new generation of believers had grown up among them, it was time again to enter the complete promise and claim their inheritance. Moses died, and Joshua led the way. The people went forth this time to battle. They conquered the mighty fortress of Jericho. Each tribe was given its own area of land, from which it was to drive the enemy. God had told them what would happen if they were negligent:

> But if you do not drive out the inhabitants of the land, those you allow to remain will become barbs in your eyes and thorns in your sides. They will give you trouble in the land where you will live. (Num. 33:55 NIV)

To each of us, as born-again believers and joint-heirs with Jesus, that time of honesty comes. We do not have 100 percent, total possession of our "self" land for Jesus. We have left some giants in the "land," and they have become thorns in our flesh. We have not fulfilled the Lord's desire and come away from all that distracts. We have not been completely dethroned. We have left areas of the Kingdom unpossessed. We still have the desire for Jesus to be King, but not the will for this. Yet the choice remains ours. God does not drive out the enemy (old habits and long-formed attitudes) before us. We must choose to do it.

One of the greatest strongholds we need to conquer is the stronghold of the mind. Before our new birth, the mind was the only safe control. To release that control is to fight a mighty Goliath, but:

> The weapons we fight with are not the weapons of the world. On the contrary, they have divine power to demolish strongholds. We demolish arguments and every pretension that sets itself up against the knowledge of God. (2 Cor. 10:4-5 NIV)

(Did you ever have a good argument with yourself about something you know you should do but keep arguing yourself out of? For instance, the need to apologize to a friend you've wronged, when you just can't admit to being wrong?)

> And we take captive every thought to make it obedient to Christ. (2 Cor. 10:4, 5 TAB)

The King James version renders "demolish arguments" as "casting down imaginations."

Imagination

Imagination seems to be our worst enemy. It is an area where Satan can trick and deceive us. He can even back up the imagination with lying emotions. How many wives have trouble with imagination when a husband is three hours late coming home from work? The imagination is so strong it can project images on the screen of your mind. The thoughts come rapidly: "He's stopped at the bar again, probably picked up someone and they are at her place right now."

Or consider what a husband's thoughts might be when his wife isn't home when he calls. His imagination can have her in bed with the milkman. Again, because of movies and television, our imaginations become overactive and the enemy sets us up. We need to come against those high places in our minds. Today we do not have idol groves concealed in high places like the Israelites did (Lev. 26:30; Num. 22:41; 23:3). The idolatry and high places are in our minds. We can be born again in our hearts and still possess unregenerate minds. We have to possess our minds for the Lord. We meet many failing Christians who are not living victorious lives because they center on the stumbling blocks obvious to other believers. Many do not smoke, drink, swear, etc., but they live totally defeated lives because of the secret thoughts not taken captive. It's time to allow the Holy Spirit to search inward, exploring those hidden chambers and tearing down the idol groves of imagination.

One area so harmful to marriage which has come to light over years of counseling is the imagined "lover they did not marry." Some actually become married to the other person in their mind's eye. Unhappiness has destroyed many homes because of these imagined relationships. Real life brings the reality of marriage—a partner with the disposition of a bear, a Scrooge, or a partner who is unreasonable, stubborn, or obnoxious (I'm sure you are adding a few). The imagination lets us escape into a fantasy relationship that totally fulfills every expectation of what we fantasize that marriage is all about. It works that way with teens and their parents. The imagination gives the right kind of loving, always sympathetic parents. This thinking is very destructive. It keeps division growing in whatever relationship is involved, whether it be parents and children, teens and parents, husband and wife, or relationships outside the family. As long as we choose to let the imagination run wild and uncontrolled, none of our relationships will be victorious and completely fulfilling.

Jesus said through Paul that we are to demolish every stronghold, to take every thought captive and make every thought obedient to Christ. The choice remains ours.

Communication is a vital key to overcoming imagination and healing relationships. To lay down my life for someone else, I need to step over my fear of rejection and to voice what my imagination is dictating. When voicing my suspicions (of those things I imagine others to be doing or saying), I must do it in pure heart love and not in judgment or condemnation. How does a wife approach a husband without putting him on the defensive? By having a pure heart attitude. The enemy plays on imagination and gives the feelings to back it up, because from these imaginings and feelings he can cause us to develop attitudes of bitterness, resentment, jealousy, envy and hatred. When the attitudes are formed and they remain and we speak forth from that place, the other person immediately puts up a defensive shield. So check your attitude before engaging your mouth, so that you might reap a good consequence.

The Israelites, when facing the Promised Land for the first time, said, "The people who live there are powerful. . . . We can't attack those people; they are stronger than we are." Sometimes, when we begin to take control of an imagination or fantasy, our attitude parallels their cry. We believe it is too strong for us. At this point, some develop a passive stance because of repeated failures. Jesus has given us complete victory in Him through His shed blood. By His stripes we are healed. Our victory and deliverance still come by way of obedience to His Word and His will. At times when we've taken a step towards obedience and failed, we become remorseful instead of repentant. Remorse is simply feeling sorry for self, self-pity, putting self down for not conquering. It is totally turning inward. Repentance, on the other hand, is turning away from self and toward God with honesty of heart, admitting our failure and trusting the control of the Holy Spirit to produce the fruit needed for our victory (Gal. 5:22, 23). As a result, we trust, rely, and become dependent on the Holy Spirit. Our imagination has been in control for a long time, and it will not be put down easily or give up easily. Victory is progressive; it depends upon our obedience in taking our thoughts captive to the Lord.

The Lord gave me a little picture one time when I was dealing with a particularly frustrating, nagging, recurring thought. He showed me himself as a policeman standing in front of a cell door in a prison. He was the jailer, and I was simply to take my thoughts and give them to Him. He opened the cell door, threw the thoughts in, shut the door, locked it and then stood guard outside the door. With Him in front of the door, the thoughts could not get out. I had to choose to let go of any fantasy life in my mind. I had to release my fantasies and give up the hiding places in my mind. I came to the truth that I fantasized, gave up the pleasurable feelings and chose the reality.

Honesty, obedience, and trust in the control of the Holy Spirit were the progressive steps to liberty from my bondage.

It is sad to see and hear from some who have mates who refuse to leave their wrong, negative thoughts and be free. So much damage and hurt to others are caused by continuing to dwell upon the lies of the enemy and taking these thoughts as truth.

Truth is that which sets us free.

> Oftentimes a Christian fails to touch truth and falls into falsehood instead. He is deceived and bound by falsehood. He does not clearly see the true character of a thing; yet he considers himself clear.[1]

Husbands, do you judge your wives as controlling your life, spying on you, checking your every movement? Do you begin to imagine her thinking you are out with other women? What do you do about your thoughts? Do you ever in honesty confront your mate? Do you keep those thoughts inside and resign yourself to life as it seems? When you choose to keep silent, resigning yourself to life as it is, you open up your home and your wife to the enemy's attacks on her mind and imagination. Little things the other person does

---

[1]Watchman Nee, *Spiritual Reality or Obsession.*

then become magnified and add to your suspicions. Wives, how about you? What negative, destructive thoughts are you carrying around in your mind? When we carry these thoughts and allow feelings to back them up, they become obsessions. To believe a lie as truth, to be wrong about a matter and convince ourselves we are right, is obsession. An obsessed person cannot be convinced that he is wrong.

We read in Ephesians 6:12:

> For our struggle is not against flesh and blood [husband against wife, wife against husband; young people against parents; boss against employee and vice versa], but against the rulers, against the authorities, against the powers of this dark world and against the spiritual forces of evil in heavenly realms.

Satan is our enemy and he is the enemy in our marriages. No Christian marriage is free from this enemy. We need to face spiritual reality and stop fighting with the flesh-and-blood mates we were given. God did not make a mistake, and you will never have the perfect mate which you fantasize that you need to fulfill your desires and longings. The mate you have is the one God will bless and join you with completely if you can come to truthfulness and honesty.

When negative thoughts come, don't resign yourself to live your life as a martyr by accepting the thoughts. You will be able to convince yourself that these thoughts are true, because your mate will have weaknesses to back up any thoughts you may have. The enemy sees to it. You then live the life of a "noble martyr" and convince yourself just how good you are to live such a hard life. Satan is out to destroy and demolish. Stand against him as the enemy, not against your mate, your child, or your boss. Come out of spiritual darkness into truth and holiness. Face the giant by laying down your life for another, and choose to communicate, no matter how right you think you are. Tear down every stronghold of the enemy!

Fears
Fear, for some, goes hand in hand with the imagination. Fears, like imagination, have feelings at the core to back them up. Fear may manifest itself in a feeling that runs very deep, fed by the thought of what might happen (the unknown), or by an actual experience locked in the subconscious. Certain situations trigger thoughts that cause the fear to surface, causing a continuing state of anxiety, dread, or terror. This too is a dreaded giant in our land that we do not like to face because of the emotional pain it brings. We do not

like walking into painful memories to take care of a Goliath, for fear of being hurt further. If we let the giant remain, it will forever be a cruel thorn in our flesh. To walk away leaves the territory unpossessed and the enemy remaining. Jesus asks us to go in and possess by dispossessing the enemy. God's way is to face the enemy (the fear), face the pain and come away the victor. He knows the power of the mind to magnify and its tendency to be easily deceived. He knows that the mind can take a falsehood and become obsessed with it until the mind believes the lie to be the truth.

The various fears in our lives block our relationships with others, especially blocking our coming to an intimate relationship with our Lord. Because fear is a feeling, we must turn our attention to the mind that feeds it. Honesty is the key to unlock the door to the mind and bring relief and release to the emotions.

One friend of mine had deep insecurities and fears of rejection. She developed defensive living habits. She would set up a shield and wall to protect herself. The shield was in her imagination. She projected in her mind the belief that she was unliked and unacceptable. This attitude caused those around her to react defensively. She had developed to some degree a masculine outlook and temperament. Because of her active imagination, she would by her own behavior set people up to reject her.

Through much prayer and seeking the Holy Spirit to uproot the root and core of this behavior problem, the Lord graciously revealed its source. Before her birth her father had wanted the baby to be a boy. He bought boys' toys and had a boy's name picked out. The day came for the baby's arrival, and it was a little girl. As she grew, her father never accepted her as his little girl but treated her like the little boy he desired. He even took her feminine name and gave it a masculine form by adding "boy" instead of "girl" (as in "Linda-boy" or "Janey-boy," etc.). When it came to potty training, she even tried standing like a boy instead of sitting like a girl.

Through the process of faith-imagination, my friend relived several specific times when she felt that, because she was a girl, her father rejected her. In faith-imagination a person, through prayer and under the Holy Spirit's guidance, brings a memory to the screen of the mind. Usually he is observing the very thing that caused the pain or trauma. This time, though, Jesus is invited there to set the wrongs right. Jesus brings healing to the memory, restores the relationship, and brings peace and forgiveness. After my friend faced these hurtful areas and came into forgiveness of her father, of herself (for being a girl and not a boy like her father wanted), and even of the Lord, she came into the total healing of her mind.

At that time, in her mind's eye she became that little girl again, but now she was in a pretty dress, not in boots and jeans. She was back at the point of potty training, sitting on the toilet, in a cute little dress, a bow in her hair, with her little legs swinging happily. There was now a total acceptance of being a woman. She could now let others accept her as a woman because she too accepted her femininity.

This same woman had to face the possibility of having contributed to the early death of her husband, because of the fears and insecurities which she had projected toward him. Our fears can cause others inward problems as well. Our own bitterness, resentments and hostilities can and do affect those who live around us. If we constantly belittle someone, putting them down with negative verbal abuse, it is like striking a physical blow. Our Lord tried to explain this when He said:

> You have heard that it was said to the people long ago, 'Do not murder, and anyone who murders will be subject to judgment.' But I tell you that anyone who is angry with his brother will be subject to judgment. (Matt. 5:21, 22)

The Lord knew the power of anger and the direction it takes toward others.

We are reminded over and over to be rid of malice. Malice is an attitude of heart that can produce intentional harm to others. It is an attitude, a heart-felt desire for injury or specific ill-will. It is spite. Having these attitudes is like constantly dripping acid on the emotions of those toward whom the malice is directed. In Ephesians 4:29-32, we are told that this attitude of heart grieves the Holy Spirit:

> Do not let any unwholesome talk come out of your mouths [what comes out of our mouths originates in our hearts, established in our minds], but only what is helpful for building others up according to their needs, that it may benefit those who listen. And do not grieve the Holy Spirit of God, with whom you were sealed for the day of redemption. Get rid of all bitterness, rage and anger, brawling and slander, along with every form of malice. Be kind and compassionate to one another, forgiving each other, just as in Christ God forgave you. (NIV)

We do carry attitudes within us that come from our fears. Whether the fears are of rejection, of being hurt, or of bodily harm, we may derive certain attitudes from them. The people we live with stimulate and feed these fears by certain things they do and say. This reinforces our attitudes. We need to look truthfully within and take captive these harmful attitudes. When directed toward others they can and do affect them emotionally and physically.

In a marriage there can be a very subtle form of dominance that sneaks in and causes another to wither and dry up instead of blossoming and blooming into life. In my friend's case, she was (not intentionally or consciously) getting even with her father for his nonacceptance of her by constantly belittling and putting down her husband. She wanted him to be stronger than he was, but he proved to be weak and then became the object of her contempt. All this time she loved him, but from her innermost being there was directed toward him a malice that caused a physical problem he did not have the strength to choose to overcome.

All of this happened in their lives before Christ came in to become Lord. Only when Jesus became a part of this woman's life and the progressive work of the cross began to produce fruits of righteousness did she become aware of these things in her life. Only as the Holy Spirit began to heal her and free her from her fears and anxieties did she see what her attitudes had caused in others. We too need to come to this realization, come into His forgiveness, and come to understand His Word to us:

> But now you must rid yourselves of all such things as these: anger, rage, malice, slander, and filthy language from your lips. Do not lie to each other, since you have taken off your old self with its practices and have put on the new self. . . . (Col. 3:8 NIV)

It is so easy to lie to each other for self-protection against our fear of rejection. When a husband (or wife) comes home and says something out of anger because he's had a hard day at the office, we form an inner attitude of hurt. Later, he is all rested and becomes little-boyish and apologetic. Now, from the hurtful place we come back with an expression such as "Oh, that's okay," when the truth is, "That hurt me, and really you weren't nice at all." Because of our fear of rejection, we lie and bury the hurt, which produces a fruit of some kind.

Consider the hurt as a seed. That seed, when buried, germinates and produces a crop. Sometimes that crop is bitterness, or anger, or rage, or malice. When I am hurt, my hurt can produce an attitude of wanting the one who hurt me to be hurt back so that he or she can see how it feels to be hurt. That is a form of malice which the dictionary defines as being, "a desire to injure (hurt) another; a specific ill will." My will is for them to be hurt too.

> Therefore, rid yourselves of all malice and all deceit, hypocrisy, envy, and slander of every kind. . . . Finally, all of you, live in harmony with one another; be sympathetic, love as brothers, be compassionate and humble. Do not repay evil with evil or insult with insult, but with blessing. (1 Pet. 2:1; 3:8, 9 NIV)

Again we must use our own volition to choose to conquer this giant in the land and dispossess him.

Anxiety

Anxiety is a disturbance of mind regarding some uncertain event, some misgiving, or some worry. It is a tense, emotional state of mind, backed by a feeling of fear, usually about an uncertain future. To some, anxiety is a giant, while others seem to have no worries at all! They are the ones who turn around and wonder, "What's the problem with you?" Fear and anxiety seem for some to be intertwined and interwoven. The mind is involved with anxiety while the emotions are involved with fear. My imagination can feed them both. Again we see the importance, when born again, of coming into the renewing of our minds:

Do not conform any longer to the pattern of this world, but be transformed by the renewing of your mind. (Rom. 12:2)

One of this world's most harmful patterns is the humanistic view which holds that there is no God and that all of man's needs for survival are met by man himself. It is from this twisted philosophy that modern psychology draws its conclusions. This view tells us that we are not responsible for our actions, that others, environment, and peer pressures are to blame for our behavior problems.

Anxiety, as it relates to our Christian walk, most commonly involves a concern that our salvation is shaky, in view of the habits that still persist and hang on. Again and again we see a stream of people who have no victory over these anxious thoughts about their future in Christ Jesus and His acceptance of them. Because of continued lack of victory over some constant, besetting sin—a habit, attitude, or weakness of character—they doubt their security.

We need to realize that our walk with the Lord is one of continuance in faith; it is a walk of *perseverance.* We need to have an attitude of persistence and steadfastness. When I became a born-again believer I was placed in Jesus Christ, a new creature—a new *creation* (2 Cor. 5:17). My sins are no longer counted against me (2 Cor. 5:19).

It took God six days to complete the creation of the universe, so we see that it was a continuous, progressive act. Not everything was completed in one day, with one grand finale. Each day was a progressive step. When by faith I received Jesus' death and shed blood as payment for my death penalty, He became my salvation. My faith in Him is one of countinuing on:

> Being confident of this, that he who began a good work in you will carry it on to completion until the day of Christ Jesus. (Phil. 1:6 NIV).

It is by faith that we receive Jesus and are hidden with Christ in God (Col. 3:3; 2 Cor. 5:17). We are kept by the power of God through faith in Christ Jesus (1 Pet. 1:5).

As we continue our life of faith in Christ Jesus, the Holy Spirit begins a persuading work within us, to bring about a change in our nature, our character, and our attitude of heart:

> And we, who with unveiled faces all reflect the Lord's glory, are being transformed into his likeness. (2 Cor. 3:18 NIV)

Some who begin to experience this correcting, disciplinary inner working of the Holy Spirit become anxious about the assurance of their salvation. ("I must not be a Christian, I keep doing . . . I can't seem to help myself.") We need to continue steadfast in our faith in Jesus' redemptive resurrection power and His Word, even while the inner work of the Holy Spirit is uncovering the trash in our lives. Every time He uncovers something, either it brings about in us an attitude of true repentance or it results in remorse and guilt, which result in anxiety, worry and the like.

Remember that true repentance turns us totally toward God and what He has done for us if we but have a heart to receive His free gift. Remorse is only a feeling of sorrow which turns us inward to feel sorry for ourselves and be filled with self-pity.

The warning to the Israelites, when they entered their land to possess it, was to totally eliminate the enemy. If they did not choose to do so, God would leave the enemy to become a thorn and a snare.

We see many Christians today with "barbs in . . . [their] eyes and thorns in . . . [their] sides that give them trouble where they live" (Num. 33:55). Have you experienced this? Can you relate to it? Jesus will not give us the easy, instant deliverance we go about seeking—only because if He instantly delivers us we will still continue in the sin or problem that brought about the bondage.

Do you seek an easy way to liberty through deliverance? What is the enemy in your land that you feel is too strong for you? Come to the heart attitude of David as he stood when all Israel quaked:

> The Lord, who delivered me from the paw of the lion and the paw of the bear will deliver from the hand of this Philistine [giant]. (1 Sam. 17:37 NIV).

After stating his trust because of earlier experiences with the Lord, David stood confident in his continued faith in the Lord to be with him in this present crisis. He was a puny adolescent, standing in front of a giant warrior, well-equipped for battle. David was defensesless and unprotected, and he has only a slingshot and rocks. Totally impossible—the mind would convince us immediately about the odds against this situation. If we approach the enemy in our own strength and protective measures, we find that anxiety and fear prevail and bring defeat. We have to choose to face the enemy like David did. He did not let the anxiety and fear cause him to hide like all Israel. He became vulnerable, exposed and defenseless. His only hope and help was in his God.

Our hope is in our Lord Jesus Christ. If we will make the stand and take an action (David threw a pebble), all the power of God, our Creator, backs up that action of faith and trust in God's power. We can stand and see the salvation of our Lord.

Progressively, daily, the Israelites walked through their land to possess it and to dispossess and dislodge the enemy. Daily, we too need to dispossess our enemies and possess this self for the Lord. The journey is continuous for all of us who love the Lord and who have our hope in Him. We need to keep our minds stayed upon Him, and:

Do not be anxious about anything, but in everything, by prayer and petition, with thanksgiving, present your requests to God. And the peace of God, which transcends all understanding, will guard your *hearts* and *minds* in Christ Jesus. Finally, brothers, . . . whatever is pure, whatever is lovely, whatever is admirable—if anything is excellent or praiseworthy—think about such things. (Phil. 4:6-8 NIV)

7

We Can Be Complete in Him

Now all the people perceived the thunderings and the lightnings and the noise of the
trumpet and the smoking mountain, and as
[they] looked they trembled with fear, and
fell back and *stood afar off*. And they said to
Moses, You speak to us, and we will listen,
but let not God speak to us, lest we die. And
Moses said to the people, Fear not; for God is
come to prove you, and that the [reverential]
fear of Him may be before you, that you may
not sin. (Exod. 20:18-20 TAB)

In our lives today we have Jesus, who wants to
bring us to meet our Father God. Our Father's
heart desire is still to have an intimate personal
relationship with each of us, His children. I
believe we get all excited and eagerly approach
this relationship, only to come to a halt and stand
afar off.

Since the Father desires this relationship, He

starts to prove us and try us, so that we might have this reverential fear (this awesome wonder of His person), so that we might not sin. What happens with most of us is that, when the testings and trials come to free us from our bondages, we start centering in on self and on the sin. Then, when the Father wishes us to draw near, we can't, because we see only our sinful selves. We fear His wrath upon us instead of understanding that we are hid in Christ Jesus (Col. 3:3). At this point, some of us choose to stay in guilt and condemnation and pick another mediator. Usually it's a pastor, counselor or friend whom we choose to be the one to hear God for us. I believe that at that time the bondage becomes permanent until the relationship is restored with the Father.

In Colossians 2 and 3, Paul points us to the truth of our liberty in Jesus:

> As you have therefore received the Christ, [even] Jesus the Lord. (TAB)

When we say "Lord," we are declaring Him to be the only divine ruler and authority in our lives. We give up our own rights to rule.

> [So] walk—regulate your lives and conduct yourselves—in union and conformity to Him. Have the roots [of your being] firmly and

deeply planted [in Him]—fixed and founded in Him—being continually built up in Him, becoming increasingly more confirmed and established in the faith, just as you were taught, and abounding and overflowing in it with thanksgiving. See to it that no one carries you off as spoil or makes you yourselves captive by his so-called philosophy and intellectualism. (Col. 2:6-8, TAB)

This warning readily applies to today's humanistic views and teachings:

And vain deceit—(idle fancies and plain nonsense), following human tradition—men's ideas of the material [rather than the spiritual] world—just crude notions following the rudimentary and elemental teachings of the universe, and disregarding [the teachings of] Christ, the Messiah. (Col. 2:6-9 TAB)

We cannot leave God's Word and choose another mediator without creating for ourselves a greater problem of bondage. Some who go to pastors for counsel are led right back to liberty because the pastor chooses to turn them back to Jesus, to repentance, and freedom from the bondage to guilt and condemnation. However, not all counsel is godly. Much of it reflects modern humanistic points of view and should not be followed. Such counsel keeps us bound to self-centered, materialistic ways and does not lead us to the Lord Jesus and to communion with our Father, who is waiting for us. When turning to friends, we have to be careful to find out where they really are in Christ Jesus. If they have no strong foundation or steadfast faith, their help will be like throwing a sinker to a drowning person. Seek the Lord with all your heart, not letting guilt and fear block or separate you from Him. As Paul tells us in Colossians 2:

For in Him [Jesus] the whole fullness of Deity (the Godhead) [to know Jesus is to be brought to the Father], continues to dwell in bodily form—giving complete expression of the divine nature. And you are in Him, made full and have come to fullness of life—in Christ you too are filled with the Godhead: Father, Son and Holy Spirit, and reach full spiritual stature. And He is the Head of all rule and authority—of every angelic principality and power. In Him also you were circumcised with a circumcision not made with hands, but in a [spiritual] circumcision [performed by] Christ by stripping of the body of the flesh [the whole corrupt, carnal nature with its passions and lusts]. [Thus

you were circumcised when] you were buried
with him in [your] baptism, in which you
were also raised with Him [to a new life]
through [your] faith in the working of God
[as displayed] when He raised Him up from
the dead. And you, who were dead in trespasses
and in the uncircumcision of your flesh—
your sensuality [unduly indulgent to the
appetites or sexual pleasure. Pertaining to
the body of the physical senses; also fleshly;
carnal; opposed to spiritual], your sinful,
carnal nature—[God] brought to life together
with [Christ], having (freely) forgiven us all
our transgressions; Having cancelled and
blotted out and wiped away the handwriting
of the note (or bond) with its legal decrees
and demands, which was in force and stood
against us—hostile to us. (Col. 2:9-14 TAB)

Satan wants us to languish in fear and doubts.
These Scriptures show us that in Jesus we have
liberty from the bondages of sin. Our sins have
been blotted out. Even if we do fail our Lord and
sin daily, we are told to confess and be forever
forgiven (1 John 1:9). We have liberty through
truthfulness with God and ourselves. Bondage is
rationalizing or reasoning that our sins are not
really sins and that they harm no one. We cannot
expect them just to go away. We need the action

of confessing them honestly. Satan and demon powers have been disarmed. They have no power! We are free in Jesus! We need not be bound by Satan's lies or by the destructive, negative thoughts he implants in our imagination, for:

[God] disarmed the principalities and powers ranged against us [Hallelujah!] and made a bold display and public example of them, in triumphing over them in Him and in it [the cross]. . . . Let no one defraud you by acting as an umpire and declaring you unworthy and disqualifying you for the prize, insisting on self-abasement and worship of angels, taking his stand on visions [he claims] he has seen, vainly puffed up by his sensuous notions and inflated by his unspiritual thoughts and fleshly conceit, And not holding fast to the Head, from Whom the entire body, supplied and knit together by means of its joints and ligaments, grows with a growth that is from God. (Col. 2:15, 18, 19 TAB)

He proves us with tests and trials, so that we might better grow to maturity. He does not discipline and prove us just to put us down or to prove that we are worthless. He wants our sinning to cease and our heart to respond totally to His love. He does not want us to keep with-

drawing and standing afar off from Him.
Paul continues in Colossians,

> If then you have died with Christ to
> material ways of looking at things and have
> escaped from the world's crude and elemental
> notions and teachings of externalism. (Col.
> 2:20 TAB)

("Do your own thing—whatever turns you
on—If it makes me feel good I'll do it—Please self;
no one else will," etc.)

Why do you live as if you still belong to the
world?—Why do you submit to rules and
regulations? [such as], Do not handle [this],
Do not taste [that], Do not even touch
[them], Referring to things all of which
perish with being used. To do this is to follow
human precepts and doctrines. [Isa. 29:13.]
Such [practices] have indeed the outward
appearance [that popularly passes] for wisdom,
in promoting self-imposed rigor of devotion
and delight in self-humiliation and severity
of discipline of the body, but they are of no
value in checking the indulgence of the
flesh—the lower nature. [Instead, they do
not honor God] but serve only to indulge the

flesh. If then you have been raised with Christ [to a new life, thus sharing His resurrection from the dead], aim at and seek the [rich, eternal treasures] that are above, where Christ is, seated at the right hand of God. [Ps. 110:1.] And set your minds and keep them set on what is above—the higher things—not on the things that are on the earth. (Col. 2:20-23; 3:1, 2 TAB)

Since we have died with Christ and are risen, we share in His resurrection power. When we keep our minds directed daily toward higher things, we are simply reminding ourselves that our citizenship is in heaven with Christ. We are strangers here; we are only on a journey to our homeland. Each experience while we are here is for our learning and growing. When the experience pertains to people, we need to remember Ephesians 6. We are not fighting against flesh and blood but against Satan and demon powers. They are already defeated and are only lying to us. Our greatest weapon is the warfare of prayer. We need to pray always and bring our petitions to Jesus in faith, believing—believing that He is God and that with Him all things are possible (1 John 5:15; Mark 10:27).

Paul tells us again,

For [as far as this world is concerned] you
have died, and your [new, real] life is hid with
Christ in God. (Col. 3:3 TAB)

As we are brought before the Father and we
stand in His presence, we are safe, because we are
hid in Christ Jesus:

When Christ Who is our life appears, then
you also will appear with Him in (the splendor
of His) glory. So kill (deaden, deprive of
power) the evil desire lurking in your members—those animal impulses and all that is
earthly in you that is employed in sin: sexual
vice, impurity, sensual appetites, unholy desires, and all greed and covetousness, for that
is idolatry [the deifying of self and other
created things instead of God]. It is on
account of these [very sins] that the [holy]
anger of God is ever coming upon (those who
are obstinately opposed to the divine will) the
sons of disobedience. Among whom you also
once walked, when you were living in and
addicted to [such practices]. But now put
away and rid yourselves [completely] of all
these things: anger, rage, bad feelings toward
others, curses and slander and foulmouthed

111

abuse and shameful utterances from your lips! Do not lie to one another, for you have stripped off the old (unregenerate) self with its evil practices, And have clothed yourselves with the new [spiritual self], which is (ever in the process of being) renewed and remoulded into (fuller and more perfect knowledge upon) knowledge, after the image (the likeness) of Him Who created it. (Col. 3:4-10 TAB)

In the meantime, while all this change is taking place, let's learn to be able to turn our faces up to our Father with a heart full of praise, trusting totally that we are in good hands.

Liberty we have been given already. Bondages come when I choose to listen to the enemy and fail to call him at his lies.

To remain in liberty and freedom, I must build on the solid rock—Christ Jesus. Stay in God's Word; hear it and learn to actively obey it. Hearing is not good without the action of obedience. God told the Israelites,

You have seen what I did to the Egyptians, and how I bore you on eagles' wings and brought you to Myself. Now therefore, if you will *obey* My voice in truth and keep My covenant, then you shall be My own peculiar possession and treasure from among and above all peoples. (Exod. 19:4, 5 TAB, italics mine)

The Israelites had journeyed with the cloud of God's presence to guide them on their way for three months. Now the cloud stopped at Mt. Sinai. Moses went up to God, and the Lord told him to prepare the people for the next two days so that they could come and meet their God. This was not to be just the usual manifestation of the cloud of His presence, which they had been daily following. Now the Lord God wanted to speak to them personally.

He said, "I bore you on eagles' wings and brought you to myself." His desire was to talk with His chosen special people, to lead and to guide them. All the people responded, "All the Lord has spoken we will do." They prepared themselves to meet their God. What they saw was not what they wanted; what they heard they didn't like.

They heard thunderings and a great trumpet blast. They saw lightnings, and felt an earthquake shake the place. From this awesome manifestation, God spoke. The people had come near to their God. He began to share the commandments, the Law of God, with them.

He spoke like a father addressing children He knew everything about. His heart was saying, "I know that inside each one of you is the tendency and will to have idols in your life; you'll desire things to fulfill you and not remember me. I recognize your anger, which so easily goes to hatred, and your instinct to lie and protect yourselves. I sense the greed that drives you not even to rest for one day and remember it was I who brought you forth. I see how you form attitudes against your parents and their needs when they're old, and how that what others have you covet and want. When those desires and attitudes do surface, this is what I want of you" (see Exod. 20:4-17). *"Keep my commands and be my special people."*

Now, when they realized that God knew their innermost beings, that He knew what their attitudes and thoughts were all about, they did not want to stand so close. When they perceived that God knew so much about what they were truly like inside, how could they draw near and live? So they all backed off and said, "Moses, you speak to us, and we will listen, but let not God speak to us, lest we die."

The desire of the Father has never changed. He still says to us today, *"Don't you remember what I did to the flesh, that old carnal nature* (Egyptians)? *It was nailed to the cross and pierced through. You were borne up on eagles' wings and brought safely to me. You can come without fear, and you don't have to stand afar off. Christ died for you; you won't be killed."* We are hid with Christ in God.

In Matthew 5, we find that when Jesus saw the

crowds, (1) "He went upon the mountain, . . ." and (2) "He opened His mouth and taught saying, . . .

> Do not think that I have come to do away with or undo the Law and the prophets; I have come not to do away with or undo, but to complete and fulfill them." (Matt. 5:17 TAB)

Not all has changed, and we cannot relax our attitude toward God's commands. Jesus went on to say,

> You have heard that it was said to the men of old, You shall not kill; . . . But I say to you that every one who continues to be angry with his brother or harbors malice [enmity of heart] against him shall be liable to and unable to escape the punishment. (Matt. 5:21-22 TAB)

Jesus came to fulfill the requirements of the Law. There was a death penalty imposed upon all who could not keep the entire law. Jesus paid the penalty—He died. Now He says the New Covenant is:

> I will put my laws in their minds and write them on their hearts. I will be their God, and they will be my people. . . . For I will forgive

their wickedness and will remember their sins no more. (Heb. 8:10-12 NIV)

He has not changed, and neither have we. We are sinners. The closer we come to God, our Father, the more He allows us to see our inner selves. He is still saying to us today, *"I know everything about you; you are weak and sinful, and your hearts are desperately wicked, but I have taken captive the enemy and killed it and have borne you to myself. Come and don't stand afar off in fear. I bore you on eagles' wings and brought you to myself."* He is still saying to us, *"My desire is for you to draw near and let me speak to you in your hearts and minds. You are my very special people, the jewels in my crown. The closer you get to me the more you will see yourself for who you really are, and then you'll know exactly the price I paid for you. I've covered you—go free."*
Commune with your Father, come close and sit at His feet. Learn to become His little child and sit on His lap. He desires you with all His heart. Prayer is our link and our lifeline. In all things, no matter what you are facing, bring Him your sacrifices of praise and thanksgiving. He cares, He loves, and He forgives. Ask Him to give you a heart to receive all He wants to give to you. Liberty is yours for the choosing!